RECOMMENDATIONS

"Carla calls us gently, but with sincere passion, to listen and respond to the whispering of the Spirit. Each devotional coaxes the reader to pause, ponder, and participate. Whether alone, with a trusted friend, or group study, these entries bring comfort while also challenging the reader. It's refreshing to discover that there are those who still listen, share, and spur us forward in our journey toward hope." — Stacey Blaido

"If you are committed to deepening your relationship with the Lord and are looking for a biblically based devotional to reflect upon during your quiet times with God, chances are you'll find what you're looking for with this 40 day devotional. Each day's message includes a "whisper" to reflect on, a prayer to help you come before the Lord, as well as the occasional heartwarming story to deepen your understanding of the "whisper" in which to meditate. This devotional is a great tool to use in your quiet time with the Lord and is sure to strengthen your faith and spiritual life." — Heather Simpson

"Sshhsh! Carla Wicks invites us to listen to God's whisper, to hear with our soul. Sharing this 40 day journey with her enriches your faith and deepens your relationship with Jesus." — Dr. Dale Schultz

"This devotional is encouraging, transparent and page-turning (but you should only read one a day)! You are being invited on a journey of growth and revelation. It reminds us to be hopeful because we are not alone. We matter to God." — Myra McQueen

"I am so honored to write a few words about Carla Wicks and this new devotional. The year of 2020 was more than we ever thought we would experience. So many have felt disconnected from friends and family, even the family of faith. Quiet and rest are vital, not only now as we refocus our lives, but always as we walk with our Savior. We so often ignore those "whispers" God wants us to focus on. We also spend so much of our prayer time talking and not listening it is hard to hear that "still small voice." This is a lovely devotional to take time each day to rest, be still and listen to the whispers of the Father."
— Pam Tidwell

that still small Whisper
40 day devotional and prayer guide

Carla Wicks

that still small Whisper
Copyright © 2021 Carla Wicks

ISBN: 978-1-7354093-0-6
(Carla Wicks /Motivation Champs)

All rights reserved. No part of this book may be reproduced or transmitted in any form or by any means, electronic or mechanical, including photocopying, recording, or by any information storage and retrieval system, without permission in writing from the copyright owner.

The book was printed
in the United States of America.

To order additional copies or bulk order contact the publisher, Motivation Champs Publishing. www.motivationchamps.com

Holy Bible passages quoted taken from Biblegateway.com:

The New King James Version. 1982.
(NKJ) Nashville: Thomas Nelson

New Living Translation (NLT) © 2015
by Tyndale House Foundation

The Message, (MSG) © 1993, 2002, 2018
by Eugene H. Peterson

The New American Standard Study Bible (NASB) © 2020
by the Lockman Foundation

The New International Version, (NIV) © 2011
by Biblica, Inc.

The VOICE translation (VOICE) ©2012 Thomas Nelson, Inc.
© 2012 Ecclesia Bible Society

English Standard Version (ESV) text 2016 © 2001
by Crossway Bibles – Good News Publishers

ACKNOWLEDGEMENTS

I give all the glory to God for birthing a passion in me for writing and storytelling. My love and devotion to God is paramount in my life. I love relating to others and using everything, the good and the bad in my life, to encourage, inspire, and transform others on their own journey.

I also want to thank my writing mentor, Eva Marie Everson, for taking a novice many years ago and instilling principles to help hone my craft.

This book would not be possible without guidance from Motivation Champs, Dominick Domasky, and his team.

DEDICATION

This book is dedicated to my husband, children and grandchildren. I love each of them beyond words. They have supported and encouraged me in so many ways. My life is richer because of each of them.

CONTENTS

Day 1	PRAYER	13
Day 2	REST	17
Day 3	CONSECRATE	19
Day 4	WISDOM	23
Day 5	GRATEFUL	29
Day 6	RIGHTEOUSNESS	33
Day 7	FAITH	35
Day 8	PURE	39
Day 9	EMBRACE	41
Day 10	HUMBLE	43
Day 11	FUNCTION	47
Day 12	HOPE	51
Day 13	GRACE	53
Day 14	IMITATE	57
Day 15	JOY	59
Day 16	ANTICIPATION	63
Day 17	ONE	65
Day 18	COMPLETE	67
Day 19	FREEDOM	71
Day 20	PROMISE	75
Day 21	BELIEVE	77
Day 22	POSTURE	83
Day 23	COURAGE	85
Day 24	MERCY	89
Day 25	LOVE	93
Day 26	FAMILY	97
Day 27	GROW	101

Day 28	TRUTH	103
Day 29	WITNESS	105
Day 30	HEIRS	111
Day 31	GIVE	115
Day 32	QUIET	119
Day 33	GIFT	121
Day 34	PEACE	123
Day 35	JESUS	125
Day 36	VICTORY	127
Day 37	TEACH	133
Day 38	COVENANT	137
Day 39	OBEY	141
Day 40	DECLARE, BAPTIZE, and TESTIFY	145
	Final Thoughts	153
	About the Author	155

INTRODUCTION

A few years ago, I invited a few friends along on a 40 day journey. I started right after Thanksgiving leading up to Christmas. We didn't travel by car, instead it was reading a daily devotional, short prayer, and a sprinkling of true stories. I had no idea how the project would fare. I read some scripture, listened to my heart, heard God "whisper" a word, said a brief prayer, and added life stories on occasion. I grew in my faith and looked forward to each day and the "whispering" God would provide in my private quiet time. These "whisperings" I discovered were meant for not only me and my friends, but for everyone.

I decided to publish the "whisperings" as a devotional and prayer guide.

From my many Bible courses and having survived the school of hard knocks, I offer these writings to you, my reader. I pray you relate to the whispered word and reflect on how it pertains to your life. My stories, both personal and offered by family, are included to encourage and inspire. From our family to yours, my heartfelt desire is a community will evolve where everyone can touch another with a "whisper."

After experiencing so many difficulties and disappointments this past year of 2020, it's wonderful when we can pause and purposefully nourish our spirit and soul. Deviations from normal life for most of the year made my quiet time even more vital. We are the generation who traversed 2020 with a lot of change. I know everyone can relate to the biggest challenge: "Expect the unexpected."

Prayer is very important for me not only in my quiet time but several times through the day. Many people have shared with me their intimate struggle with how to pray and what to pray. Sometimes, words escape us, we can't vocalize our needs or concerns and emotions run high. We find ourselves sitting in silence. I have learned over the years that a great starting place to grow your prayer life is to pray as our Lord modeled and use scriptures. There are no better words than those in the Bible. Any time we use the Word of the Lord as our source material it is music to God's ears. The Lord's Prayer and the 23rd Psalm are two of my favorite examples. I use one in the morning to start my day and the other as an evening prayer before bed. Day one and two of this devotional provide insight into both of these prayers. I have expanded the language to make them personal for me. Feel free to modify as you see fit to make them your own.

WHY A 40 DAY DEVOTIONAL?

- It's a good start to form a wonderful habit. Anyone can take ten to fifteen minutes each day to just be still and listen. The most wonderful blessings for me have come when I was disciplined to listen, *only* listen. No talking on my part, I want to hear in my heart what the Lord desires to speak. I encourage you to try it.

- Scripture is full of important events in regard to the number forty. The children of Israel wandered in the desert for forty years. Moses was on Mount Sinai for forty days and nights, twice, seeking the presence and glory of God. There are forty days of Lent. There were forty days from the day Christ rose from the dead until he ascended to Heaven, just to name a few.

So, come along for the next 40 days and enjoy these "whisperings." I want this devotional to be a starting place for everyone to experience "whispers" from the Lord. May the Lord meet you mightily as you devote time in His presence. It is my hope you will have many experiences with our Lord and build your own treasure trove of whisperings. Journal along the way so you can revisit these precious moments.

WHAT WILL YOUR 40 DAY JOURNEY LOOK LIKE?

It will be very different for each person. Everyone will read and ponder the same word "whisper" and yet the diversity of reactions and responses will be as personal as your fingerprint. I'll bet you experience some brighter days ahead. Remember, your "whispers" have a twofold purpose:

- They bless you and bring hope and strength.

- You are the channel God uses to reach others when you walk in faith.

I offer the following daily devotionals and pray they are a blessing and you become a whisperer to someone in need of hope. I am a whisperer, and you can be too.

DAY 1
PRAYER

Breaking down the Lord's Prayer reveals more than simple words. I never understood that there was a pattern. If I could follow said pattern and personalize it, then The Lord's Prayer would be specifically effectual.

I will share some important insights I have learned over the years, from my Pastors at Gateway Church, Robert Morris and Jimmy Evans, in regard to the Lord's Prayer.

In Matthew chapter six, Jesus is instructing on Prayer. His example for us begins in verse nine.

OUR FATHER IN HEAVEN – Acknowledging first thing by *doing so* (action) with much thanksgiving, praise and worship.

HALLOWED BE YOUR NAME – He and only *He* is the authority. His name is sacred and higher and more powerful than any other.

YOUR KINGDOM COME, YOUR WILL BE DONE ON EARTH AS IT IS IN HEAVEN – We need to have our mind set on kingdom living and bringing that into our lives.

GIVE US THIS DAY OUR DAILY BREAD – He is provision for everything we need here on earth. Through His divine favor, we can rest knowing He sees what we need.

AND FORGIVE US OUR DEBTS (sins) AS WE FORGIVE OUR DEBT-

ORS (those who sin against us) – Forgiving is releasing, untying, and removing from our yoke those with whom we have issues or have an issue with us. Knowing Jesus intimately, we realize he will work this for our good.

AND DO NOT LEAD US INTO TEMPTATION, BUT DELIVER US FROM THE EVIL ONE – We need Him to show us the way, direct our steps, shield us from harm and provide protection for us.

In some Bibles, the Lord's Prayer ends here. But there is a final stanza.

FOR YOURS IS THE KINGDOM AND THE POWER AND THE GLORY, FOREVER, AMEN! Matthew 6:9-13 NKJV – We finish the prayer as we started, by acknowledging He is divine and His kingdom is the right way to live. We declare it all by faith. This is our proclamation and we end with a powerful — Amen.

The Lord whispered *prayer* to me as the beginning of this devotional because it is an ongoing state of being for the Christian person. We are instructed to pray without ceasing. It's like breathing, our way of constantly staying connected to God.

So, I offer what I have learned and experienced. I want to be found faithfully sharing, a conduit. To get us started I offer to you my personalized Lord's Prayer.

MORNING PRAYER – THE LORD'S PRAYER

Good morning my Daddy, Abba, Father who art in heaven, sitting and ruling above everything and existing simultaneously everywhere. I'm thrilled you are not limited by the bounds of earth. Hallowed is your name, which is most sacred to me and worthy of all my praise and thanksgiving. Your kingdom come and your will be done, here on earth as it is in heaven, where you rule and have established your authority as King of Kings. I'm constantly abiding under your protective covering and am subject to your will in and for my life. May your perfect kingdom come with power and engage my heart to bring about your unique purpose in my life. As I yield to your authority, I can resist the devil. Give to me this day, and this day alone, my portion of your daily bread through mercy and favor. I submit to you the desires of my heart and all my concerns I have this day knowing you will carry them for me. I release the burden and weight they represent. Forgive my debts as I forgive those who are in debt to me. I ask forgiveness from your throne of grace for anyone I have wronged, whether knowingly due to my human failings or unknowingly. I speak blessing over anyone who has wronged me and give him or her into your hands. While I count on you to strengthen me against temptation, if I find myself there, deliver me from evil. I thank you for exposing the works of the enemy and am confident you are faithful to keep me from harm. I believe in your perfect protective pillar of fire to guard my property, my family and myself. I am grateful you are the warrior I need when there is trouble, seen and unseen. Be my shepherd and send mighty guardian angels to surround me wherever my feet trod. I thank you for today and that you care so diligently for my family when unexpected situations arise. We are blessed being grafted to your side and under your massive wings. For yours is the kingdom, the power and the glory forever. Everything I am will always remain for you alone; your holiness expressed through me as Lord of my life. I will never take glory for myself, as nothing in this life is about me. Everything is about Jesus. Holy Spirit, be present in power with me this day, as I can do nothing without you. Amen.

that still small *Whisper*

DAY 2
REST

When each day is done there comes that peaceful time of rejuvenation and rest. Even God stopped when He created the world in order to rest. There are benefits to our spirit and body when we take time to rest, thoroughly and completely.

Complimenting Day one, I want to give you my evening prayer so you can begin to make it your own as well. He whispered the word *rest* to me. In order to sleep well I must turn my thoughts to Him at the end of every day.

Keeping these prayers printed on cards near me, by my bed, to start and end the day, allow me to stay focused on the Lord. I need Him before I rise and as I lie down.

EVENING PRAYER – THE 23RD PSALM

The Lord is my shepherd and my relationship is, and always will be, that of his dependent child. I shall not want for you, Oh Lord, have supplied me with everything I needed this day. You make me to lie down in green pastures, give me rest, and renew my physical body. You lead me beside still waters where I find nourishment from the water of your Word, which quenches my thirst. You restore my soul and bring healing to my physical body, the temple where Your Holy Spirit resides. You guide me in the path of righteousness and in doing so have ordered my steps to line up with your Word. For your namesake, I will commit to the plans and purposes you birthed in me. Even though I walk through the valley of the shadow of death, by means of trials and testing in my life here on earth, I trust in you alone to deliver me. I will fear no evil because you are the ultimate protection I need. For you, Lord, are with me, ever faithful and true to the promises I keep in my heart. Your rod and staff comfort me and bring the needed discipline I require to grow as a child of yours, as a living example of Christ in the world. You prepare a table before me in the presence of my enemies giving me hope that will never fail all the days of my life. You anoint my head with oil, as I stay consecrated to you from the day of my salvation and new walk of life. My cup overflows with the abundance of your grace which I need every day. Surely goodness, mercy and love will follow me all the days of my life because you bless those who bless your name. I will dwell in your ultimate security and in the house, you have prepared for me, Lord, forever and for all eternity. Amen.

DAY 3
CONSECRATE

The whispering and rumbling in my heart this morning was *consecrate*. I like the definition "to dedicate to a divine purpose."

I went to the Word and decided to read and ponder Romans 12:1-2. Paul is writing and instructing on how to live in holiness. It must begin with a choice to offer and place before God your entire body as a living sacrifice. Deliberately focus your mind and attention on God. Ephesians 4:23-24 talks about letting the Spirit of God renew your thoughts and attitudes so that your new nature will reflect outwardly. Then, a person can know and be able to discern what God calls good, pleasing and perfect. Transformation happens when you can immerse, flood and cover your mind with the truth.

As I worship the Lord, it requires of me to have a fixed (fastened securely in position) mind. A mind that is not swayed by what I hear or see in this world but rather by what I read and hear in my heart as truth from the Bible.

Lord, I make a choice of my will to offer you my entire body, all of its parts. I ask for you to speak to my mind, your truth. Shine your light and help me walk in a new attitude and behavior. I desire for my outward reflection to be one, which pleases you. Amen.

Can you dedicate your body to the Lord for His divine purpose? How does the transformation look to those around you? What happens when light envelops you?

Let me share a personal story.

I worked as a dental hygienist for many years. One day, I had a patient who the staff told me not to engage in conversation. The patient grumbled constantly and was mean. I was instructed to just clean her teeth and dismiss her. I immediately asked the Lord if he would provide a door of opportunity, I would be obedient to engage in conversation.

The patient arrived, her body rigid and her face contorted and hardened. Moments went by with not a word spoken between us. She knew I noticed the poor condition of her mouth. She suddenly spoke, saying, "It doesn't matter, and nothing matters anymore!"

I took this as an open door and ventured in by saying, "I had a time in my life when nothing mattered. It was when my son died."

Her eyes shot open; she stared at my face as she grabbed my hand, stopping me from working. "What?" she said.

I went on to tell her the story of when my whole world changed. I told her after my initial grieving time I knew I had a choice. I could die within myself or I could ask God to help me use the experience for good.

Her eyes penetrated me. She slowly began speaking, "My son died too, and I've never been the same. I can't find the way forward and don't know how to go on with my life. I am angry even though I don't want to be."

I stopped what I was doing, kick shut the door to my operatory and sat her upright. I didn't know what I was going to say next, but I knew what I had to do and that was to place my arms around her and allow her to cry. Cry she did and cry I did.

We drenched each other's shoulders. We said not a word, but our hearts were speaking volumes back and forth as one mother to the other wept for our sons. When we broke the embrace. I saw with my very eyes a transformed countenance. Light had entered her darkness where she had been stuck for fifteen years. I knew in that very moment if my son had died for no other reason than for this encounter, with this one woman, it had been worth all the agony and anguish I had endured.

Our Lord died and if he died for no one else but you He says it was worth it. How wonderful. How marvelous. How divine. I can't imagine not giving Him my body, TOTALLY as a living, breathing, walking, talking instrument. You?

that still small *Whisper*

DAY 4
WISDOM

This morning I chose to read James 1:1-12 (NLT). Many consider the book of James the Proverbs of the New Testament. It is full of sound information on how to apply principles of living, which are tied to spiritual truth.

In verse four it uses the phrase "perfect and complete." Understanding it is our patience, married to endurance and perseverance, which makes us mature, perfect, complete and able to finish the race.

The whispering word today is *wisdom*. I decided to look it up to see if my understanding of wisdom was correct. I had always believed that wisdom came from journeying life, with lessons learned from everything we encounter. Been there, done that, and have the t-shirt, ya know? That makes you wise, right? James understood wisdom to mean the manner and skill to live life with excellence while making good choices and decisions. Anyone can attain wisdom, and at any age, but you have to ask God to give to you.

Trouble and trials in life are not a matter of if they will happen, but when. Stuff will happen, we can be sure of this. Our response needs to be unwavering, not moved and never wondering <u>IF</u> God will help us through. <u>WHEN</u> we ask God for wisdom, as stated in verse five, He is ready, willing and excited to give it to us. This increases our faith and our single-minded conviction and assurance. He will handle the situation and bring us through. Our faith is related to our relationship with God. Staying in tune with Him, always seeking Him daily, is critical because He is the only teacher of wisdom. Those who don't ask must feel they don't need divine teaching, right? How many times have we all tried to handle something within our reasoning and understanding?

Stay convinced and believe wholeheartedly that your faith will be radiant under pressure. Be sold out and never doubt God will provide His wisdom to you and allow you to arrive at good decisions. Seek him daily and ask. Never forget—depending on Him for divine teaching will level your mind from turbulent thoughts so you can stay the course and finish the race of life…. WELL. Pray, believing! Be expectant!

Lord, I want my mind fixed on you and totally convinced at all times and in all things that you are there and will provide me all the wisdom I need. I need the wisdom of your guidance and direction each and every day. Help me to never go it on my own. Infuse my mind with your wisdom as I stand in faith, believing and totally convinced of your love, which is always for my ultimate good. Amen.

Allow me to share a story from my husband, Ken, in regard to seeking wisdom and following God's plan.

At age sixteen, most boys are thinking about sports, girls, or getting their driver's license. My son, Donovan, was focused on becoming a United States Marine. Since I was a closet helicopter parent, and our country was in the midst of a war in Iraq, I was not thrilled about the idea of my son risking his life in the conflict. Don't misunderstand me, I'm very patriotic and come from a patriotic family. But this was my son…my *only* son.

My military veteran wife was doing her best to support Donovan's choice without shooting down my suggestions for other career options.

Over the next couple of years he regularly worked out at the gym with the Marine recruiter, the recruiter's father (a retired Marine), and other young men with the same goal. Naturally, I offered alternate career suggestions. I would say, "Let's check out Texas A&M and make a visit to the campus. You could be part of the Corp there while getting your degree."

At one point I abruptly burst into his bedroom and declared, "I have just two words for you." He looked at me with a surprised face as I staunchly proclaimed, "Air Force". I felt surely that would be a safer choice. Those Marines are the tip of the spear. My overly, protective father mode, was anxiously looking for options that would be less risky, yet still appeal to him. None of my suggestions deterred him, and he was laser focused on joining the Marines.

Donovan's eighteenth birthday was upon us. This is the age, when we call someone an adult in our country. One is able to make their own decisions without parental consent and able to direct their life's path. However, I felt he lacked wisdom and experience that come with age. I thought, "Ha, what do these kids know at age eighteen?"

Off he goes to the MEPS in downtown Dallas. This is where all the branches of the military enlist and get sworn in. He said he would call to let me know how it went. I began praying in earnest, asking God that if this was His will for my son, then He would let him be accepted. I got news about lunchtime that they weren't satisfied with his spinal exam and were sending a Marine to our chiropractor's office to get his x-rays. He did have a hereditary spinal curvature. I thought to myself, "This could be the deal breaker," but I continued praying the same prayer. If it was the Lord's will then he would get in, if not, he would be rejected. Temptation was strong to ask God not to let him be accepted, but despite my strong leanings. I knew that would not be right.

The day seemed to drag on forever and I finally got a call from Donovan around dinnertime. "How did it go", I asked with great anticipation.

He said they still were not happy with his spinal condition and sent him out to a doctor in downtown Dallas for more x-rays. Despite his borderline condition, Donovan was accepted in the Marines. I told him of the prayer I had been praying all day. Then he said something that totally surprised me. Actually, it shocked me knowing his resolve to enlist. He said to me, "Dad, I've been praying the same prayer myself all day".

That's when it happened. Something that felt like a burst of power downloaded on me, causing me to literally take a couple steps backwards as I still held the phone up to my ear. I heard the Lord say, "Be careful you don't get in the way of what I'm doing." Immediately I saw a picture in my mind of my son, standing sideways and slightly looking up, with Father God looking directly at him. As they looked at each other I had an amazing, yet disturbing feeling of being someone looking in from the outside. This was the Lord, Donovan's creator, looking intently at His son, with Donovan looking back at him. Sure, I knew I was his father too, his earthly father. But God was clearly impressing on me that He was in charge of his life. I wished He would have also said, "and by the way Ken, I won't let anything bad happen to him".

My sense of trust was being tested. I realized that I had been given the awesome gift, and responsibility, of raising this fine young man, yet ultimately God was THE FATHER.

The days after that were quite different. I became his biggest cheerleader. I had the "Marine Dad" hat, the "Marine Dad" bumper sticker, the "Marine Dad" shirt, etc. This experience changed my entire outlook on all my children. I still had as much zeal to teach them, protect them and guide them down the correct path, but I was able to do it with open hands, trusting the Lord. My helicopter had landed. No more hovering over all of them to make sure everything would turn out perfect, just the way I thought it should.

Well, Donovan made it through his years in the Corps, his deployments to the war zones and other places. God is faithful. There will always be parental challenges. Once you're a parent, you're a parent for life. I've wanted to take off in the helicopter a time or two, I must admit. Yet I'm confident and relying on The Father's most profound wisdom to maintain the higher view of his children.

that still small *Whisper*

DAY 5
GRATEFUL

My daily reading the Word continued in James 1:13-18. I was especially moved with verses seventeen and eighteen. This scripture reference is talking about gifts given and received. God is consistent. Our job in His plan: Live by His message of truth to show the world His goodness and love. His whispering, *grateful*, calmed my heart. I was weepy. I have so much to be grateful for when I look at the world and the hardships many endure.

Lord, I thank you for every gift you have given and those you are yet to give. I even thank you for those things in my life I might not call good or perfect, yet I have confidence you are and will work them for my good. I fix my mind firmly to your work in and through me. I am grateful, so very grateful. Amen.

Let me share a personal story. I made reference in Day three about losing a child. He was my firstborn son. He was in the US Navy at the time of his death. I was allowed to fly to Reno, Nevada, the site of the accident, to see him before they proceeded with organ donation surgery.

The walk down the hallway of the Medical Center from the elevator to his ICU room was one I will never forget. Nothing prepared me for standing at his bedside as he lay there strapped to more tubes and mechanical devices than I thought possible. The sounds were amplified in my head and all I could do was stroke his arm and the sides of his face. Oh, how I longed for his eyes to open and for all this to be a horrible bad dream. As I stood there saying my goodbyes, I didn't see any way this could ever work for my good. My son, so full of promise, was gone and any chance at life was over. I kissed his face as my tears wet his pillow. I left that room with a huge hole in my heart.

Fast-forward twelve years. One morning as I sat alone in my kitchen, my mind drifted to Paul and how much I still missed him. I got defiant with the Lord and demanded to know what possible good I would see from this huge void in my life. While I was grateful for my other children and family, I was missing him terribly. I begged the Lord to hear Paul's voice one more time, see his smile, know he was doing fine. I sat for what seemed like hours waiting for the Lord to answer me. I closed my eyes and all I felt, was as if I were in a dark box. I struggled to find the light anywhere. I was about to open my eyes when I got this sensation on my cheek, just a hint of a touch. Then a few words in my heart, a whispering, "I am here, this close, and have every tear you have shed." And the darkness was gone.

I cried. The whole experience left me in awe and in peace. I've had many a conversation with God and know without a doubt this one special moment was for me. I got to experience closeness with the Lord I could only have had due to the huge heart wound I was enduring. I demanded He meet me, and he was faithful. While I never condone demanding of the Lord there are times in all of our lives when we want a taste of his glory so bad, we get bold.

Since then I have been even more grateful than before. I live with an attitude of gratitude because I know it pleases Him. Every time I read the account of Moses and his experience seeing the backside of the Lord from the cleft of the rock, I remember that touch on my cheek. To this day I can't adequately describe it to anyone. I knew in that moment I had his assurance he knew the depth of my pain. It was all I needed to carry on, blessing others and telling them the most important truth they will ever hear this side of heaven. **God is closer to you than you think, and he walks with you every day.**

I wish each of you, my readers, a bountiful grateful day, harmony with those around you and love expressed with kindness, compassion and mercy.

that still small *Whisper*

DAY 6
RIGHTEOUSNESS

This morning I continued reading in the book of James. Life hit me, ouch, in the first verse. "Don't get worked up into rage so easily…" James 1:19 (VOICE)

To me *righteousness* was whispering in my heart. I was seeing over the past few days what Christ in us should look like to the world. The scriptures were showing me Jesus in a practical application for my daily living. I could see how to take what I was reading as truth and when applied it would transform and correct behavior. I could live like the Master intended.

I see where we are instructed to first—listen, second—harness our desire to speak and finally be slow to get angry or enraged. Notice it doesn't say don't get angry instead says be slow to anger. There are examples in the Bible of many, including Jesus, who were and did display anger. The goal is to do the first and second part *before* displaying the emotion.

Lord, I want to live in right standing with you and only display the character I desire to be. I accept, as a human, I fail daily to live it out, as I should. I must and do depend on you to quicken to my heart when I should be listening more. Help me be patient and to only speak what I hear the Spirit of God saying in my heart. Forgive me when my mouth engages and erupts. Help me to become a better listener. Amen.

One Thanksgiving Day, my ovens heating coil decided to catch fire and burn in half. My turkey was half done and the first of my three casseroles were headed into the oven. My initial reaction, after getting the fire out, was not a pleasant one. The words from my mouth were not kind and life giving.

For years I have struggled with a Martha complex. (You who identify know all too well the struggle.) You are either the Martha, who has everything in order, scheduled and controlled or you are a Mary, who goes with the flow with hardly a care in the world.

Well my Martha kicked in with a vengeance.

I had to get my turkey to a neighbor to finish the last hour of cooking, the corn and green bean casserole had to go on our grill (thank goodness we had one) and the sweet potatoes had to be fried on the stove. Everything worked out with our meal only a bit delayed. The meal was very nice.

Now, if I had been a Mary we would have forgone the casseroles and turkey, eaten a meal of deviled eggs and cranberry sauce followed by pumpkin pie and called it good.

So this morning when I opened my Bible and read the first verse about being slow to anger I took that for me as a whisper to work on righteousness (or my lack thereof). God was getting my attention and saying, "I know you were upset the meal didn't go as you planned. What wasn't so *good and perfect* was how fast you got upset followed by an unharness mouth." I'm just keeping it real for everyone.

We get several opportunities to exhibit what our human nature is capable of as evidenced by how we carry ourselves. I realized, more than anything, why I need His wisdom to make the good decisions in both my actions and my speech. I think consecrating my ears to listen so they bridle my mouth will keep me pointed in the right direction, with Jesus holding the reigns.

DAY 7
FAITH

My scripture reading for today was James 2:14-20 (NIV) and it spoke of faith and works I know a lot of people that exhibit one or the other. The challenge is doing both and in the manner scripture states here.

Verses fifteen and sixteen give us a story example. "Suppose a brother or a sister is without clothes and daily food. If one of you says to them, 'Go in peace; keep warm and well fed', but does nothing about their physical needs, what good is it?"

Verse fourteen says, "What good is it, my brothers and sisters, if someone claims to have faith but has no deeds? Can such faith save them?"

Verse seventeen adds, "in the same way, faith by itself, if it is not accompanied by action, is dead."

And verse twenty drives home the point, "you foolish person, do you want evidence that faith without deeds is useless?"

Here are two different translations of verse twenty, "Faith without works is useless" (NASB) and "Faith has to show itself through works performed in faith." (VOICE) The latter one made me go back to Hebrews 11:1 where faith is defined. Again, two translations: "Now faith is the assurance of things hoped for, the conviction of things not seen." (ESV) And "Faith is the assurance of things you have hoped for, the absolute conviction that there are realities you've never seen." (VOICE)

The Lord whispered *faith* and it spoke volumes.

A word study taken from Hebrews states, technically, "appropriating what God in Christ has for man, resulting in the transformation of man's character and way of life."

For me, doing those things (works and deeds) from a pure heart of compassion relate to the transformed life one has when they are in Christ. Our spirit will actually yearn to "want to do" those things. What do you think?

Lord, show me daily where I can use my faith to help others. Allow me to hear you speaking clearly. I desire to have you use my entire consecrated and transformed body to do those things you have for me to do. Amen.

Faith is an all-encompassing term and gets thrown around so much in regard to many things. I wanted to dig deeper and see if I could grasp it even better. I found a passage in Romans 3:21-28 (NLT) which combines it with right standing with God. Listen to the repetitions in verse twenty-two, "We are made right with God by placing our faith in Jesus Christ." Then in verse twenty-five, "We are made right with God when we believe that Jesus sacrificed his life, shedding his blood." Then in verse twenty-eight "We are made right with God through faith and not by obeying the law."

So like we talked about yesterday with righteousness we see here that by faith we hold fast and believe and that posture makes us right with God.

What other passages can you find on faith that speaks to you?

I'll share a story from the fall of 2005. Our family was living in a nice subdivision and I had volunteered to serve on the HOA board as the newsletter person. On August 29th a category four hurricane slammed into New Orleans. I watched the daily news stories from the comfort of my home. I was moved by the horrendous amount of destruction and so many displaced with no home. Many people were relocated to our Dallas/Ft. Worth area.

I heard from a friend about a family who sought out goods from a local shelter and I got an idea. There was a duplex down the street so I contacted the realtor handling the property and asked if I could rent it for a displaced family. I then used our community newsletter to alert my neighbors for help with monetary donations, food, clothing, and furniture.

The end result we were able to move the family in, fill the fridge, furnish it and pay for three months of rent. It felt good to help in whatever small way we could. The family was so shocked to see a neighborhood pull together and bless them. The blessing on our end felt even better.

that still small *whisper*

DAY 8
PURE

The whispering I hear today is *pure*. As I continued my reading in James 3:13-19 it speaks to clarification about God's wisdom and how it's related to our works and deeds. I can see where it mentions in verse fourteen to make sure our heart is not jealous or selfish and not covering up or proud by lying or boasting.

I'm sure you may know those who do good things and will make sure others know they have done good things. They simply cannot let the action go unrecognized. Whether they are attaining accolades from others or drawing attention to the deed themselves, the Word cautions us to watch the intention in our heart. What is the motive of our heart and actions? If we carry out faith filled activities in a pure, peaceful and gentle manner than we know we are exhibiting Godly wisdom and our good fruit is not filled with hypocrisy.

Verse eighteen sums it up with how we can reap a life full of righteousness when we plant peace filled seeds.

Lord, guard my heart and mind. Help me to use your wisdom in all my actions. As I walk out my consecrated life, in you and with you, keep selfishness far from me. Allow others to benefit from gifts you want to bestow through me as pure and lovely. Amen.

How many ways can you find to be pure (complete and absolute) in your actions to others, coupled with good fruit? Can you recall a time where you were of service to another out of a heart of compassion?

DAY 9
EMBRACE

The whispering I hear today is *embrace*. As I was finishing the book of James, I was captivated by James 4:8 (VOICE). One translation says, "Come close to the one true God and He will draw close to you. Wash your hands; you have dirtied them in sin. Cleanse your heart, because your mind is split down the middle, your love for God on one side and selfish pursuits on the other."

I found it interesting that it says to *wash* our hands, *cleanse* our heart because our *mind*… The body part connection is fascinating. Our mind is split, divided and going in different directions, our heart needs cleansing because our hands are dirty.

I think as humans we have a difficult task of keeping our mind stayed, focused and directed toward God and His desires. Due to the world in which we live, move and breath it is ever in our face. Does this challenge any of you? How are you meeting the task of not having a divided mind?

I love when I can get in a quiet place, pray, and listen to what the Lord is dropping in my heart. I often hear whispers and sometimes it's assertive and direct. Like I mentioned before I'd love to be like Mary and just sit at Jesus feet. ALL. DAY. LONG. I have work to do, though and so the "stuff and things" are right there waiting for me when I leave my quiet time.

Lord, help me to be <u>mindful</u> of those things I do and give my attention to every day. Are they kingdom or are they worldly? Guide me with your wisdom to be where I need to be, doing what I need to do, speaking life, and shining your light around me. Amen.

When I imagine coming close, or drawing nigh as the King James translation states, I think "embrace." To stay in a constant embrace with Jesus would help to shelter me from so much. Being in His embrace would allow my heart to beat in tune with His.

Was there a time when you were drawn to something worldly even though you knew or found out later it wasn't something that brought you peace?

DAY 10
HUMBLE

I've been reading in Luke 18:10-14 (NIV). A portion of verse fourteen has been quoted from pulpits, repeatedly. The whispering I hear is *humble*. "…those who exalt themselves will be humbled and those who humble themselves, will be exalted." It speaks to actions we control. One is to bring us into line for feeling more highly of ourselves than we should and the other, to reward behavior that doesn't puff us up. I don't know about you, but I prefer to not exalt myself. I would much prefer to allow Him that privilege.

I looked up a few words for their exact definitions as I was pondering the word humble in my quiet time. Look at what I found:

Humble: a modest or low view of one's own importance.

Self-esteem: confidence in one's own worth or abilities.

Confidence: a firm trust, belief that one can rely on someone or something.

What stood out to me is that anyone can have a very healthy self-esteem (having a *firm trust* in their own abilities and worth). As long as the confidence is in who is important, God, not us. In and of ourselves we are nothing. We can only be empowered to do good works and deeds by the one who gives us our abilities. As we daily present ourselves, humbly, before Him then He will raise us up — exalt us in those gifts, talents and abilities, which were given by Him to us. It's all about Him! Ask Him where to use what He has given you, being careful to never think more of yourself in the process. We are His extension, conduit, and channel (hands, feet, mouth, and body) to bring the world what He desires.

Lord, I want to praise you for the specific talents, abilities and gifts given to me. They are not mine alone. They are for others. Help me to keep my confidence in you as I walk in those things you desire for others. May I always give you credit, not taking any as my own, for the outcome of blessings others experience when I am an extension of you. Amen.

Even more today than when we started ten days ago, I acknowledge He who is the giver of the talents. I am thrilled I get to use them for others. Those abilities, which are a passion in me, I give Him full credit. I am pleased they burn in my heart until they are expressed where they bless others.

What passions, talents and abilities has the Lord given each of you? How are or can you use them to bless others?

I always say it is easier to see a talent in another than in myself. I can spot the gifting's on people's lives and am more than happy to pray with them for those things to come to pass in their life. On the other hand, I struggle to identify my purpose. I know the things I am passionate about and the things I feel are talents, but I wonder where they fit in the kingdom purpose for my life.

Fast-forward about five years. I started discussing this with a few friends and someone said, "Why don't you write a book?" While I love writing and have taken courses to improve, I never saw that as my offering, until recently. It wasn't until I did some blogging with a small group of ladies that I realized the degree to which they were blessed. My friends in turn began blessings others.

This very book is my offering. I don't want to be heard. I want readers to hear God. I have prayed over each entry and over every reflective personal story. I told God I would obey his leading and *write*. I am confident in him to infuse his power over the print. Being vulnerable in sharing personal stories along the way allows me to touch readers where I know many have had similar experiences. My desire is this devotional creates a family bond of readers, a sea of whisperers, who will share of themselves with others creating a beautiful aroma, pleasing to the Lord.

that still small *Whisper*

DAY 11
FUNCTION

The reading for this morning is in 1 Corinthians 12. Paul explains how the Spirit will manifest in believers for works of service. I have read this portion of scripture many times. I find more nuggets to focus on each time I read and really let it sink in and work in my life.

The whispering today is *function* (a purpose natural to or intended for someone or something). I don't know if people really inquire of the Lord and diligently seek him about the specific talents and abilities, which have been entrusted to them. Since each of us is uniquely different then it stands to reason the Holy Spirit will move in and through us each differently. Even the outward expression will be different yet when we all come together, where God has placed each one to be, it represents a whole body. There will be hands and feet, minds, and mouths, etc. Once the body is complete with all the parts assembled and functioning in their gifts, talents and assignments then we can see a glimpse of how God designed humankind, in His likeness.

The problem comes when people don't like what they are and wish they were something else. There are many who never find where they are supposed to be so their talents can be joined together to function. Many try to be other parts of the body and try to "work and serve" in several areas. They may not be called to serve in a specific area but do so out of a works mentality, to be seen, instead of inquiring of the Lord and only doing what He directs. This just causes unrest and a feeling of being lost and unfulfilled. It also takes away a place of service from someone who is rightly suited for that area.

How many times have you encountered a person and said, "They were born to do or be that!" Most likely the person has found their calling, niche and talent. They are using it and functioning correctly. This causes them to be fulfilled emotionally, mentally, and spiritually.

Be cautious of the trap, which the enemy would like to use to hinder you or all out stop you from growing. That would be the "I can do it all, or they really need me to do_____, or if I don't do it then it won't get done." I could go on and on. Ever have any of those statements run on a track in your head?

Lord, I seek your wisdom and want you to speak clearly to my heart. Show me what you placed in me before I was born which you desire for me to use to bring your kingdom to earth. Help me see how to and where you planned for me to serve. Help me to recognize opportunities and be bold <u>in your power</u> through me to do what you will. Amen.

Here is what I took away from today. I think of it in steps.

#1 Discover your gift, talents and abilities. Listen in your heart. Ask God to illuminate them so they become a consuming passion. Seek His wisdom in what He reveals to you.

#2 Ask Him what part of the body is your area of expression. Actively listen. It may not be what you think. Thank Him for what He reveals. Seek His timing and positioning for you to move into them.

#3 Ask Him where He wants you to express what He revealed. Commit your life to follow and be obedient to what He tells you. Thank Him and fix, stay and position, your mind there. Focus on the assignment.

Don't worry about the significance whether it is small or large. In verse twenty-two the *least important and weakest* were the most necessary. Something you do may be needed in order for someone else to function in his or her gift and so on.

I was not raised in a home where church attendance and biblical living were modeled. I had plenty of spiritual relatives and got fed morsel by morsel from them. Yet Christlike expression was missing on a daily basis in my home. I went to church camps as a youngster but nothing along the lines of a real encounter with God happened until I received my salvation at twenty years old.

My church going extended family members were charismatic. I heard stories about "sharing your testimony" and "praying for people to be saved." I can honestly say talking to or even worse praying for a total stranger, or friend for that matter, seemed weird and uncomfortable to me. I didn't want to be seen as "one of those people" and yet I did have a desire in my heart to let others know, by experiencing it for themselves, what a converted life was like. I just didn't know how to go about it so as a result…. I did nothing.

For years I only shared my "testimony" (personal encounter) when I was asked. I hardly ever prayed with someone, except in my own quiet time when I would mention his or her name to the Lord.

I think part of my hesitation, besides how I would come across, was the "what if's." What if I prayed for someone sick and they didn't get better? What if nothing I said in my testimony was encouragement to anyone in his or her situation? What if I didn't hold the answer, the key to unlock the solution to bring them healing, hope, and a better life than before we met?

During a church service not long ago, I heard my Pastor say something that totally revolutionized my mind concerning encounters with unsaved people. I thought that Christ through me needed to meet them, bring the solution AND witness the transformation. The full meal deal, the complete package, the signed, sealed, delivered "I'm yours Lord." But wouldn't you know what my pastor said set my mind free and has given me much more liberty. He mentioned — God calls some to plant, some to water and some to harvest.

My light bulb had gone off…ding, ding, and ding! In other words, He didn't call hardly any to DO IT ALL. Oh my, YES! That was it. Billy Graham, one of the most recognized evangelists of all time, was seen most often during harvest. In his crusades, the masses of humanity in attendance came hungry and understood miracles happened there. Why? Because Mr. Graham was faithful to do his part, with the talent he possessed and consecrated to the Lord, where he was to do it and when he was to do it. God orchestrated those hearts in attendance to either be ready for planting, or receive their watering, or for some, yes some, the full meal deal of a harvest.

Now when I am in a situation where I feel the tugging on my heart to talk to someone or pray for one another I simply ask God to use my testimony in whatever stage they are presently.

Do they need planted? Is there ground someone else tilled and I need to help him or her step into what is prepared.

Do they need water? Is there something I need to say to encourage them or pray to help them put roots further down keeping them steady, to not give up?

Or is it time to harvest? I need to share something, or an action I do will allow them to step into their own new life.

I hope this is a help to you as it was to me. It brought me such freedom to function in my sharing with others.

DAY 12
HOPE

The whispering I hear today is *hope*. While reading in Ephesians, a letter Paul wrote to the faithful followers in Ephesus, I just loved the prayer he offered daily to the Lord on their behalf (Eph 1:17-20). He had heard of their strong faith and love for God's people.

His desire for that community is the same for those of us — to have increased insight and wisdom. He understood this had to come via the Spirit as it was coursing through them with a brilliant light, increasing their knowledge of God. This would be how they would grow and at the same time their hearts would be filled with an understanding confident hope.

The Lord longs for us, you and me, and every believer to receive this hope and embrace the inheritance and full extent of His power. It is the same Spirit working in us that raised Christ. In other words, we have within us and ready to be used by us, God in His fullness. We just need to activate it, share it and move with our talents using it.

Lord, I am honored to be your child. I am blessed beyond what I can describe that you chose me to be in community with all Your Holy people. Give me tuned in ears to hear you as I move about each day. I hunger for your hope and truth. Amen.

Hope is defined as a feeling of expectation and desire for a certain thing to happen. I am yearning for hope to increase in me daily. I want to witness more of the presence of the Lord, here on earth. That is my desire for each of you as well.

It is easy to get overloaded with commitments and be lost in the hurry of "doing". Often, we pass right by someone who is hurting and fail to notice. It could even be someone putting on a happy face. May our hearts be sensitive to those we rub shoulders with and if we can offer them anything from His kingdom, may we do so.

Allow me to share a story my son, Tony wrote.

My parents divorced and in my younger years I had quite the strained relationship with my father. I always felt like I was living in the shadow of my older brother, Paul. Paul was, after all, the namesake of the family. The moment when that turned was the passing of my brother to which my mom wrote about on Day five of this devotional.

After I graduated high school and enlisted in the military, my father and my relationship became much different. I had always hoped it would but didn't dare dream it really could. Even though it was better it was still not what I would call the same as most others have with their father. My dad had a lot of issues that led to him passing at a younger age. He had those around him that helped him. There were times where our relationship would strain over his issues. We had a difference of opinions. No matter what myself or others felt about my dad's choices, those were his to make. I don't look back on the bad but only focus on the good times that he and I shared. The memories when it was good to spend time with him. My hope is he rests in peace now.

DAY 13
GRACE

Continuing my reading in Ephesians, I love how in chapter 2 there is an explanation about how much the Lord loves us. He corrected the separation sin caused. With mercy and love He flooded our soul with His Spirit. This overwhelming gesture was given by grace. We receive and walk in it by faith. Faith is appropriating what God in Christ has for man, resulting in the transformation of man's character and way of life. God longs for all of us to return to the garden.

Understanding what God does for us at salvation is to breathe on us and infuse His very nature, spirit, power, blessings and anointing in us so we can carry out what He desires as if He were here walking the earth. We can't buy it or work for it. It is not purchasable or a reward. It is free, given out of love so we are never separated from God again.

Lord, thank you for loving us so much you would give us your precious Spirit. May we be mindful everyday of your presence, we carry with us, as we go about our daily life. Help us to treasure it always. Amen.

The whispering word of today is *grace*. Grace is defined as the free and unmerited favor of God. In Ephesians 2:4-10 grace is mentioned three times. Anytime I read something in scripture and it is repeated, I take a special note of the point being made. In this case God is telling us to quit thinking we can strive for it, be good enough to get it, purchase it with enough offerings and investments. The only way to get it is to freely accept it. Adam and Eve never struggled with this concept. They were the purest form of God's created human being. They walked the earth in harmony with God — in His garden. At least they did before encountering Satan.

Now it's time to get personal. Ken is not my first husband. He is actually my third. Like I mentioned a few days ago, I did not grow up in a Christian home. By the time I was ready to graduate high school I was yearning for a new life. I thought I would find it, and the acceptance of my parents, by joining the military. I enlisted in the USAF and it wasn't long before I realized this wasn't fulfilling the yearning in my heart.

I met a man, and he had experienced a much different childhood. We married and I was experiencing the genuine love I had longed for through my new family. Problems arose and our marriage did not weather the storms.

Divorced with four children I never dreamed I'd meet anyone, let alone a man who had no children. But I did. This new admirer verbalized promises for a life I'd never known. So, we married. It was apparent to me even though I had deep affection for this person the same did not hold true for my young children. There was disharmony. I made the choice to go it alone as a single parent, rather than subject my children to an environment, which I saw no hope of changing.

After my oldest son died, I moved to Texas. I started a good job and found a great church. My life was complete or so I thought. (I will interject here. God is so good, He sees and listens to the longings of our heart. Even if you do not vocalize them, His Spirit that lives in you knows what you desire. He is constantly working in us to bring those things to pass.)

Meeting Ken, many years later, I told him my story. He knew at this point in my life I was done with marriage. I had four children I loved immensely. I was God's kid so I knew everything would be okay even though the desire of my heart to be happily married had not worked out.

With Ken, I had found a friend I could talk to even though it was by email. It just felt great to chat with another human being about "stuff." He had kids and totally "got" what encompassed the majority of my life.

We shared work stories, church happenings and mutually liked corresponding. I never dreamed it would move from that to phone calls, to meeting in person, to moving into dating. But it did. From friendship to love, the Lord guided me, taking the longings and dreams of a little girl and showing me what true love could be.

I believe my meeting Ken was not an accident it was divinely planned for just the right time. God was showing me through another individual what it meant to be loved unconditionally, be patient and kind, sacrifice and honor — all things I had given up hope would ever be mine. But God wasn't done yet.

When I was living close enough that Ken and I could see each other more often we liked to go to Ft. Worth and UNO's restaurant. We would sit at the same two-topper table in the corner. It was just quiet enough to have some great conversations. One night while we are there, I started explaining to Ken how I envisioned the Garden of Eden, if it were accessible today. I used to dream about being there. We would talk for hours about the "what if's" of us getting to live the ultimate plan A of God. What would it have been like to walk *with* God? Living with so much glory and everything in its perfect form. Could our eyes and heart be able to partake of that much beauty? Could we have withstood the enticing of the enemy to eat and partake of the forbidden fruit?

Our conversation about this subject matter stretched over many meals there. I could imagine how even today believers could experience that Eden by the choices they make. Finding a place in their home and life to yield to God where He could come and sit, move, dine and talk with us just like He did in His garden. A place devoted, consecrated and set apart where His communication is pure, sweet, not intimidated, no walls separating and nothing hindering.

Ken and I dined at UNO's so much before we married and after that it is like a second home to us. I got a crazy idea to ask the manager, now a friend, if we could place a brass nameplate on the table where we sat regularly during our dates. We shared with him our topic of many an evening pizza meal. He agreed. We got a nameplate engraved and went back on our anniversary to put it on the wall.

Ken and I both prayed for this table to be a place where God could move and hopefully entice others to conversation. The dining public may never know the full story of why it was labeled "Return to Paradise" but yet we do. We went there on our sixteenth wedding anniversary for lunch, asked for "our" table and rekindled the conversations from many years ago.

Sadly, this last year in October UNO's closed due to Covid economic issues but the manager retrieved our nameplate and gave it to us. It will always remind us of the beautiful beginning of the rest of our life.

God longs for you to return to the garden in whatever fashion possible. I can promise you some of the sweetest conversations and impressions you will encounter are there in majestic beauty — just for you.

DAY 14
IMITATE

Ephesians 5 is packed full of instructions on wise living. Sounds wonderful and perfect. However, I am sure each of us can find at least one "ouch" in the list of don't dos. I attempt to hold to as much wise living guidelines and suggestions as I can. Then I seek more wisdom and help from the Lord in my areas of weakness.

In totality the chapter's advice is there to help each of us to live outwardly in the fullness of Christ. The Holy Spirit shines and moves when we are reflecting and walking in the attributes of the Lord.

Lord, help me to grow and learn when I am exhibiting anything less than what you desire of me. I ask you to speak to my heart. I am thankful for mercy in those times when I might be tempted or do fail by speaking words or exhibiting actions unbecoming of your nature in me. I love you and want to imitate you always. Amen.

I hear many whisperings today, but I chose the word *imitate*. Ephesians 5 begins with a simple command to imitate God and follow Him like the treasured children God knows us to be. He watches over us and loves us so deeply.

Think of someone you looked up to either when you were a child or now as an adult. Who is that someone you wanted to imitate? Why? What was it about them that drew you to want to model their actions, behavior or temperament? What qualities stood out as noteworthy enough it caught your attention and you hunger to be just like them?

DAY 15
JOY

My Bible reading for today found me in Luke 15. The chapter begins with people, sinners and the worst of the lot in attendance to His parables (stories). They often came to listen. Who else was there? The Pharisees and teachers of religious law also attended. They complained that Jesus was rubbing elbows, even eating with this lot of unsavory folks. Could Jesus have shared these same stories with the elite, the learned, and the ones who felt they knew it all? Jesus knew his target audience and He knew how to reach them. Notice it doesn't say the ones complaining stuck around or were listening as if to learn anything.

Story #1 tells about a man losing a sheep, verses four and five. He searches until he finds it and when he has found it, he is joyful.

Story #2 tells about a woman losing a coin, verses eight and nine. She searches until she finds it and when she has found it calls her neighbors and friends to rejoice with her.

Story #3 tells about a man and his two sons. Verses seven and ten speaks to the joy in heaven when a sinner repents.

Take a few minutes and read the chapter and pay particular attention to what Jesus is saying. You will notice the end result of each story has the owner finding and becoming joined together again with something they lost. There is JOY!

Most people either love or hate the prodigal son story in verses eleven through thirty-one. Depending on a person's mindset, you could easily be rejoicing that the wayward son is home, having learned a lesson the hard way OR you could be wondering, like the older and more faithful son, why throwing a party is the thing to do. He was faithful and never got a party. No matter where you stand in your feelings about this story the <u>truth</u> is simply woven in all three stories.

I see the main points as this:

- It hurts, causes pain and longing when something is missing and/or lost.
- Our hearts ache until we locate and get back what we lost.
- A sense of relief washes over us when things are back where they belong.

So let me ask, why do you think Jesus started talking to this particular crowd about sheep lost and money missing BEFORE He dove into the lost son story? Did He want to gain their full attention because many of them could relate to missing possessions? He was speaking to what they currently valued. Have you ever noticed in verse twelve when the son *told* his father what he desired (his share of the estate) the father *agreed*? He didn't steal the money. According to Jewish law the division of wealth between sons was two thirds to the older and one third to the younger. Don't just assume when the father "divided" it, each received a fifty-fifty share.

Lord, I thank you for once I was lost and you looked and waited for me to find my way to you. You were there to embrace me and welcome me home. I love how your heart is constantly longing for others to find their way home. Help me to never squander your majestic wealth by passing a lost person. Give me boldness to be light everywhere I go. Amen.

The whispering today is *joy*. Joy is defined as a feeling of great pleasure or excitement. Imagine living with it every single day. I know hard times and bad things happen to each of us. The overriding emotion should be joy because we know a father who is worth getting excited about and who longs to bring us great pleasure. Joyful, because we are His kids, and His wealth is ours here and in heaven.

How are you using the wealth of the Father through the Holy Spirit? Are you joyfully giving it away?

Many years ago, I began a writing course and was paired with a successful author as my mentor. My mentor co-authored a book series called "The Potluck Club." I bought them and devoured each one. The writing elements and characters were so relatable it drove my passion to write and get published one day. Throughout the course my mentor and I shared stories. I gained a tremendous amount of respect for her and others who have gone from talking about a book to finishing. The process of writing is tedious and hard work, it takes a massive amount of perseverance. It takes stamina, commitment, and discipline.

Fast-forward a few years and I attended a Christian Booksellers convention in Dallas. I was able to meet my mentor in person. Working the booth with her was her co-author on the book series I previously mentioned. I was over the moon with joy standing between them for a picture. I was in dreamland for what this could look like for me one day, not just an author hopeful but a published author myself.

Fast-forward again several years and I am very involved with Community Theater. I dabbled with some onstage roles and then some backstage tech positions including stage-managing. One night, while running the sound and cue board, I get the harebrained idea to contact my writing mentor and her co-author about taking the first book in their successful series and try my hand at creating a stage play. Did I mention I had not written anything yet? But they both were so encouraging and told me to take a stab at it and we'd talk. (Like I said there is a long road from talking about something to actually doing it. I really think they both wanted to see my commitment to actually go the distance.)

Several months of revisions later, a group of volunteer actors workshopped the script. Then more edits and a final script was born. After the contract negotiations were drafted and signed "The Potluck Club" stage play was ready for a world premiere.

I enlisted the help of actors from my community, found a church for the venue site, and rehearsals began. A few months later, with extreme joy, the play opened for a two- weekend run. Opening night both my mentor and her co-author were front and center in the audience to see the characters they wrote about come to life. Audiences loved the show and I was more than satisfied.

The picture I have in my home with the book authors, co-authors with me on the stage play version, is very special. It reminds me of how much joy there was in finishing a dream project, coming full circle with where I began many years before.

Every single step of the project I laid before the Lord. It brings joy to my heart to see what he accomplished through me when I dared to tackle a project bigger than myself. I couldn't have done it in my own strength but with him guiding and directing me where to step and what to pen, the work found completion.

For all my community theater folks out there and church creative arts teams who want a wonderful play to perform, I can hook you up because where it goes is the Lord's to decide.

DAY 16
ANTICIPATION

Today I was reading in Philippians 3:12-17. Paul is commenting on how he walks out his life and he is encouraging the people of Philippi to do the same.

I like how he begins by (letting those who are reading or hearing his letter) stating he has not reached his goal and is hardly perfect. This is comforting because I am very far from perfect and often make mistakes, usually daily. I strive to be in the will of God doing what is planned for me. If there is angst in my life, now as an older adult, it is because I yearn for discovery of the purpose and plan for my life. Any of you feel this way?

Paul repeats what he has yet to achieve, but he has a focus. "…forgetting the past and looking forward to what lies ahead." (Phil. 3:13 NLT) Like a runner in a race he uses this example to state he is constantly moving forward, keeps going, being deliberate and making haste so that he may win the race of life and find God well pleased when he crosses the finish line. The prize is eternal life with Christ.

This is our mission, let nothing stand in our way, leaving our old life behind and running toward the things of Christ. Confidently we take each step forward to attain the goal.

Lord, help each of us to be runners for Your Kingdom purposes. May we stay the course, keep focused and encourage others to run. As we make the choice to leave behind the past, and instead look into a bright future, we know you will be there in love cheering us on with every step. Amen.

The whispering I hear today is the word *anticipation*. When I think of looking forward to something it causes excitement. I would long for each of us to be full of anticipation each day knowing there will be people and opportunities where we can encourage other runners.

DAY 17
ONE

Start today reading in Ephesians 4. You don't get very far before you see the whispering for the day — *one*. From verses four through ten the word one is used ten times. Why is it repeated that many times? Again, I take note of this repetition. Here is the list:

ONE Body

ONE Spirit

ONE Hope

ONE Lord

ONE Faith

ONE Baptism

ONE God

Each ONE of us…

The same ONE who descended

Is the ONE who ascended!

We are challenged to live our life worthy of the grace He has given to us. We can do that best by being gentle, humble, patient, kind, etc. Walking like Christ modeled will be what unites us, not divides us. We do not have to create the model for unity. Christ did that with the Holy

Spirit who has been left behind for each of us when he ascended to sit with God in heaven. We have that *grace in FULL measure*. Nothing more has to be added. There is nothing we can do to earn it. We just get to walk it out!

Lord, I long to be using my life as you modeled and in the manner you find pleasing. Allow me to use the grace with the powerful presence of the Holy Spirit, your oneness, to impact the world. Amen.

So how do you see yourself as ONE in His kingdom, sharing in his pattern for living in unity? Can you think of a time you were witness to division and something you did brought unity?

DAY 18
COMPLETE

The scripture text for today is in Revelation 2 and 3. There are encouraging verses and instruction. John is writing down his visions of what he has observed in the past and is seeing for the future.

The seven stars represent angels appointed to the seven lampstands, which are different churches in Ephesus, Smyrna, Pergamum, Thyatira, Sardis, Philadelphia, and Laodicea. Each message speaks to them of God knowing what they are going through, how they are afflicted, persecuted and under stress from spiritual things contained on the earth. There are seven different encouraging words from these messages.

- "...I have seen your hard work and patient endurance..." (Revelation 2:2 NLT)
- "I know about your suffering and your poverty (but you are rich!)" (Revelation 2:9 NLT)
- "I know that you live... you have remained loyal to me. You refuse to deny me... my faithful." (Revelation 2:13 NLT)
- "...I have seen your love, your faith, your service and ... your constant improvement in all these things." (Revelation 2:19 NLT)
- "I know... you have a reputation for being alive..." (Revela-

tion 3:1 NLT)

- "…I have opened a door that no one can close… You obeyed my words…" (Revelation 3:8 NLT)
- "You say, 'I am rich … I don't need a thing!'" (Revelation 3:17 NLT)

There are traps to overcome and commands to obey. Following these admonishments to ALL churches is the exact same announcement: *"Anyone with ears must listen and understand."*

The promises to each will be victory in God. Revelation 2:7 promises fruit from the tree of life in paradise. Revelation 2:11 promises not to be harmed by the second death. Revelation 2:17 promises manna hidden away in heaven. Revelation 2:28 promises the same authority I received from my Father given as the morning star. Revelation 3:5 promises never to be erased from the Book of Life. He will announce before the Father and angels that these are His. Revelation 3:12 promises all to be pillars and write upon all — His name. Revelation 3:21 promises all to sit with His Father on *His* throne.

The number seven is used more than seven hundred times in the Bible. Most of the times representing divine completeness starting in Genesis when creation was "completed." I think there is much we can take away from these instructions to the seven churches.

Lord, praise you for giving encouragement and also correction in our lives. Knowing you mean it for all, and to help grow us and complete us. Amen.

The whispering today is *complete* — perfect, lacking nothing. By the worlds standards we will never be complete. Thank the Lord in His eyes and by His hands we ARE perfect and complete.

Our mission going on from here is walking in His perfectness, complete in all He has given to us, which is in us by way of the Holy Spirit, our strength, guide, comforter, and wise counsel.

- Are you perfect? Not here on earth but in His eyes we are.
- Are you complete? Yes, in His love, both here and in heaven.

Look today for someone you can verbally bless by telling him or her they are perfectly complete. You will make their day and it might be the very words they need to hear.

that still small **Whisper**

DAY 19
FREEDOM

My reading in Colossians 2 this morning I found interesting and informative. If you research the lifestyle of those living during this time you will find there were rules, holy days, festivals, feast days, etc. Paul is doing his best in this letter to the faithful in Christ, followers of Jesus, to inform them they don't have to live under strict adherence as others do outside of the knowledge, baptism and faith of Jesus.

Paul says, "…don't let anyone condemn you for what you eat or drink, or for not celebrating certain holy days or new moon ceremonies or Sabbaths." Colossians 2:16 (NLT) He tells the people that these are only shadows of the reality to come and that reality is Jesus. He goes on to list more things not to feel condemned by and shines a light toward where they need to be focused. He reminds them of who lives in them now.

Fast-forward to our time, culture, habits and lifestyle. Those of us in Christ, have the anointed one living in us as our reality and ruler of our emotions and behavior. Do we fall prey to what others might try to demand of us as to our way to live life? Can you recall a time when someone mentioned, hinted at, or came right out and demanded we follow their lifestyle? Were they trying to cause you to steer in another direction? What was your reaction? Do you know of any who are trying to live a rules-based lifestyle thinking their "suffering" will gain them more rewards or jewels in their crown? Or that in their "suffering" they will find favor with the Lord after they pass from this world?

In other words — whom Christ has made free is free indeed. The only voice we need to hear is His. Only allow others to speak into our lives with life based, affirming words free of condemnation. Their motives should be pure, coming from a heart devoted to the love of Christ and His desire for His creation.

Lord, may the words of my heart, the whisperings I hear, be light and life to others. In a world of rules and opinions may your message, which originates from the throne of God, be what rules us all. Amen.

The whispering for today is *freedom*. Have you seen Mel Gibson in — oh you name it. In my opinion, his movie characters are full of expression. His shout of FREEDOM in *The Patriot* is epic. It reverberates. His portrayal of Christ in *Passion of the Christ* elicits many raw emotions.

Freedom defined means: a right to act, speak, or think as one who wants without hindrance or restraint, not being imprisoned or enslaved. Christ came to break us out of the prisons of defeat and despair. He came to give Himself so we would never feel like a slave to the world. How are we shouting "freedom" to those we connect with, have influence toward and those who seek us out for guidance, wisdom and hope? How can you express daily, to the Lord, your gratitude for making you free?

Here is another story written by my son Tony about his time in Iraq with the US Army.

Memories of my Iraq deployment began when we arrived on that foreign soil and our preparations were underway to make our vehicular road march to the location we would occupy; our area of operations.

My battalion commander stood before us and said few words. Some of the words are forever etched in my memory. He said, "If not you, than who?"

To most of the people I served with in the military it was literally that simple. We made the commitment to do that job because we didn't live in a country where you are forced into military service. We were there so the ones we love don't *have* to be there. For much of my time in that country, dealing with the rigors mentally as well as physically, you lean on things that bring you solace. For every person that's a different thing. Some have wives and children others have siblings and for some it's mom and dad. You get time to communicate with them periodically, but for a majority of time it's someone you call "brother." It's a fellow soldier who you don't need to relate to because you're both in the "suck" together.

To this day if I am on social media it's more often than not that I am reading about the lives of, not my family members, but the "brothers" I served with over there.

One buddy, Gilmore, who I met in Iraq, walked into a room where our cots and bunks had been decorated with trinkets from our loved ones back home. There on his bunk was a Kansas City Royals blanket. Despite never having met the guy, an instantaneous bond was formed because of the shared passion of a sports team. Gilmore and I, to this day, are lifelong friends and brothers. We stay in touch. I am sure both of us provided the other a sense of comfort and peace in a difficult time. We have since gone to sports events together. These are the easy stories to write about.

The tougher stories are ones that take you down a similar path but have a drastically different ending. Christopher was another guy I met that same deployment and he had a passion for Kentucky basketball. We had an instant connection because Kentucky was as rich in basketball tradition as my favorite Kansas Jayhawks. Kentucky was also the team that my father passionately followed and cheered on. So yeah that camaraderie was there and was palpable, even though we rooted opposing teams. It was a friendly bond.

Christopher deployed again and unfortunately passed while on his deployment. When you find out about these tragedies it does hit home because it's not just a name on a wall or a memorial. It's a life that intersected mine and we were friends. It's personal.

I was there when we captured Saddam Hussein; I've seen the inside of his palace as we occupied the area. I sat in my Bradley tank when mortar rounds came within inches and I've seen my share of death.

To this day it is only my "brothers" who understand. There aren't words to express the trauma to folks at home. I'm grateful my life was spared and if sharing my story helps someone than isn't that what it is all about. Helping each other?

Hearing my son talk of Iraq reminds me of my time in the Air Force during Vietnam. The stories of our military are deep with emotion. As the saying goes, freedom is NOT free. And it's true.

DAY 20
PROMISE

This marks our halfway point in our 40 days of "whispers" and finding out more about the nature of our Lord. My how time has flown by.

My morning Bible reading today was in 2 Peter 1. Simon Peter wrote this letter to other believers. He was encouraging others to grow in the knowledge of Christ. He was asking God for more grace to accomplish it.

I was thinking today of the wonderful promises we can claim as our own because we have accepted Christ. What he died to give us is indeed humbling. These promises are what give us the voice of hope and peace in a troubled and corrupt world. Verses five through seven tell us to respond with these actions to secure, claim, and walk in the promises.

- Add to your faith — moral excellence and virtue
- Add to that knowledge, wisdom and keen insight
- Add self-control and discipline always
- Patiently endure with long suffering
- Use godliness and reverence to God
- This gives way to brotherly affection, kindness and gentleness
- Finish off with love for everyone

Growing in these attributes and traits will make you very useful and productive with your knowledge of Christ in *you*. Once you see exactly how the Father sees you, and what has been given to you to give away, it will reflect and speak boldly to those around you.

Lord, thank you for giving us promises of how to grow in a divine character reflecting you. May we each day pick one and focus on it. We are grateful that our old nature is now changed forever when you entered our life. Amen.

The whispering I hear today is the word *promise*. Defined it means an assurance that one will do a particular thing or that a particular thing will happen. We can see above how our nature will change when we take on and model what is living in each of us. I like how love for everyone is the ultimate culmination of growing faith.

The Bible makes reference to faith as small as a mustard seed, how it can grow. Mustard seeds are very, very small. No matter where you are beginning, no matter how insignificant it may seem, when you add the other ingredients it multiplies and produces a heart full of love.

I have a tiny mustard seed taped in my Bible to remind me that beginnings often start small. What small thing are you ready to grow?

DAY 21
BELIEVE

Today I was reading Acts 13:42-52 (NLT). Paul and Barnabas had been sent and commanded to preach the good news of salvation to the Jews <u>first</u> before taking this message to the Gentiles.

The scene, imagine with me, begins with Paul and Barnabas leaving the synagogue. The first thing I think is the boldness they had to have in order to speak up in the religious house — preaching about Jesus, one of their own, as the long-awaited Messiah. It goes on to say *many* Jews and *devout converts* followed Paul and Barnabas. But the two men encouraged them to rely on the grace of God.

We have read other passages about grace and how we need it to grow and receive the blessings of God. Many Jews begged Paul and Barnabas to come back the next week and talk more about these things. Verse forty-four says the following week "…almost the entire city turned out to hear them preach…" Word traveled fast and you can imagine the hearts ready, like a field tilled for seed, for the teaching. Or so they thought.

Immediately we see in the next sentence the statement. Only *some* of the Jews saw the crowds (not *some* of the Jews hated the message) and were jealous; so they slandered Paul.

The story goes on. Since the Jews rejected the message, the two men preached it to the Gentiles. Many believed and converted. The Lord's message spread throughout the region. This angered the influential religious women and leaders of the city, so they stirred up a mob against the two men and ran them out of town. Having been rejected there they journeyed on to the next city with their message of the grace of God for salvation.

Isn't it interesting how fast the people were enraged? The entire city moved from a feeling of anticipation and expectation to hear Paul and Barnabas to becoming a mob, running them out of town in a spirit of rejection.

Lord, help us to never reject your grace poured out for us. May we be supportive of those you have called with the gift of preaching to lift them up as they bring Your Word and clarify it to our hearts. Amen.

The whispering today is *believe*. This is defined as having confidence in the truth, the existence, or the reliability of something. I am so happy to believe in the Word and its living power. I am thankful for those who blazed the trail, preaching the Word.

Do you know people who follow the crowd? They are swayed by what others think, say or do? In this case some believed Paul and Barnabas and it was joy for them. Others were eager to hear and could have believed but were later found amongst the masses, the mob that slandered Paul and Barnabas, chasing them out of town. This continues even today.

May each of us be light and hope to others around us who are easily swayed and not confident with an assured hope, being fixed in their faith. May we be ready to even speak one word that could be just what they need to hear to believe.

I'd like to share a story about my oldest daughter, Christina, and how she held onto believing in the face of great difficulty.

Growing up, bodies changing, it is all uncomfortable and at times intimidating. The journey is different for every young lady, some handle the monthly hormonal disturbance, others find the ordeal excruciating. It messes with emotions and creates physical pain. It is the rite of passage from adolescents to womanhood and eventually motherhood.

When my daughter said she was having horrible pain (to the point of not being able to stand or walk), I felt horrible but dismissed it and explained that pain was part of the process. This continued month after month with hardly any improvement. She had found a way to cope but it still wiped her out for a few days each month. All comfort treatments and over the counter remedies were of little help. She did what she had to do each month to get by.

After a few years had passed I was beginning to be somewhat concerned. She was still struggling and hardly improving. This was not normal. Did she have a low pain threshold? I would later in life learn how high a pain threshold she maintains.

Everything changed the month she simply couldn't move from a fetal position in bed. She was throwing up and looked beyond miserable. I got her an appointment with my OB/GYN and he suggested an exploratory procedure to see what was going on. I couldn't believe it; she was only nineteen years old

It was grueling to sit in the waiting room while they did the procedure, only to have the doctor come out afterwards and tell me he had "good news and bad news." I felt sick for not having gotten her professional treatment sooner and extremely worried at what "bad news" meant. I asked for the bad first.

He told me Christina had been born with two uteruses. I was in shock and then he explained further. It seems the tissue which would normally make one uterus had divided and made two complete organs. They sat side by side in her abdomen cavity.

Unfortunately, one had a cervix and completed the monthly cycle just fine while the other one had no cervix and malfunctioned, eliminating the discharge into her abdominal cavity. Due to this ongoing problem she had developed adhesions. Everywhere. She was suffering with debilitating and extreme endometriosis. The doctor went on to say they checked for multiple kidneys because in these cases of divided organs there are usually three or four kidneys. Luckily that was not her case.

I then asked about the good news. He was quick to tell me they could operate, remove the bad uterus, and clean up the adhesions they could see. However, he said it was like picking dandelions and they would re-appear over time. She would need multiple surgeries.

At age nineteen she underwent the first two abdominal surgeries. She was put on medication that made her body think she was in menopause to help with her healing process and prevent the monthly cycle. We would then learn more bad news. The doctor told her she would never be able to have children because the tissue, which divided and produced the double organs, meant the remaining one did not have the elasticity to carry a baby to term. Coupled with that, her chances of even getting pregnant were slim. With only one ovary present, her egg count was greatly diminished. It would be almost impossible for her to conceive. Her medical file was labeled "Pelvic Cripple." She was facing a future with no children. This was devastating.

Fast-forward five years. She met her future husband. I was excited for her and sad at the thought of her not ever being able to have kids of her own. Then came the day she told me, "Guess what, I'm pregnant."

Miraculously, she had gotten pregnant but needed constant monitoring. It also meant an absolute need for birth by c-section if she was able to get that far. There was no way her uterus could hold up to the pressure of contractions and hard labor. It was all uncharted territory and she took it month by month. No one knew how the organ would respond.

My daughter is tall and the chance of the baby being small was not likely. The month she called to tell me doctors wanted to do an abortion because during routine testing results showed the baby had Downs Syndrome. I cried. This could not be happening. The fact she was pregnant at all was God's hand and I simply couldn't believe she would have to be facing this prognosis.

But she forged ahead confident in the Lord to give her a healthy baby. She got as close to term as she was allowed and to prevent uterine rupture before labor began. Her uterus remained strong. God was faithful. She delivered a healthy baby boy with no Downs Syndrome or other complications.

Fast-forward four years. She got pregnant again and delivered a very healthy baby girl, despite bad test results early in her pregnancy, another recommendation for an abortion and her own medical issues, she stayed strong until her scheduled c-section day.

Both pregnancies found me in constant prayer. No one knew if her uterus could hold up, twice. There were too many unknowns. She frequented the doctor's office so they could watch her closely. I held fast believing in God to bring her through again.

Today both of my grandchildren, ages twenty and sixteen, are proof of a powerful God's hand. And both are very healthy. I am thrilled my daughter was able to have a family. God can and will do miracles when medical science says to the contrary.

Where do you find yourself today? Are you daring to believe God can do something powerful in your life? Do you wonder if he hears your cries, the desires of your heart? Has he given you a whisper of a promise? A whisper of something he wants to birth in you and like Abraham and Sarah you are wondering how he will accomplish his plan in your life?

I will just have you remember that with God ANYTHING is possible.

Hold onto your dreams, place them in his hands and then believe in him to move on your behalf.

DAY 22
POSTURE

I was reading John 8:1-11. It is titled, "The Woman Caught in Adultery." I'm going to ask you to look very closely at the posture of Jesus.

Verse two *He sat down* to teach them when he arrived at the Temple. As He was speaking, the religious leaders were poised and ready to spring something on Jesus. They wanted to trap Him, use His own words and actions against him. They addressed Him as teacher, then stated the offense, followed by stating the law and consequences of the day for the offense. They demanded an answer asking what He has to say in his defense. They didn't care about the woman as they were seeking to catch Jesus going against custom and law.

Verse six says *He stooped down* and wrote in the dust with his finger. A long debate exists about what he wrote, no one knows for sure. The religious leaders were demanding and insisting on an answer. So obviously what he wrote wasn't the answer.

Verse seven says *He stood up* and gave them the answer, his answer/command stated in an emphatic manner, "He who is without sin among you, let him throw a stone at her first." (NKJ)

Verse eight says *He stooped down again* and wrote in the dust. The accusers dispersed, beginning with the oldest, until no one was left but Jesus and the woman in the middle of the crowd.

The religious people brought her to Him because they had a mission — to cause Jesus to stumble in front of the crowd.

Verse ten says <u>Jesus stood up again</u> and He addresses the woman, she answers, and He sets her free.

I like to put myself in the story. In this case imagine with me you are the woman being drug out to publicly stand before the crowd and be the subject of a questioning involving Jesus, The Anointed God incarnate.

Notice how he postures to you? He was sitting when you arrive, He listens to accusations from a seated position, then bends even lower to write in the dirt (a number, a symbol, a word — no one knows). After being badgered, He stands, the position of authority at eye level and answers with an order to examine themselves first. He then goes down to the ground to write again and remains there until all the accusers of hers have departed and then he stands to pronounce her freedom.

Call me silly but if I were the woman and Jesus changed his posture like this with me, I would be moved emotionally. It is very humbling when someone assumes a lower position. He didn't invite her to kneel with him. He changed his posturing for her.

Lord, thank you for the freedom we have in your grace and mercy. When we sin, no matter the kind, you are there to pick us up, emotionally. When the world throws accusations we know our hope is in you and the love you have shown to us. Amen.

The whispering I hear is *posture*. This is defined as a particular way of dealing with or considering something; an approach or attitude. Not only can we change our physical position, we can re-posture our attitudes. Speakers speak from a standing position. Teachers teach standing, facing their students. Employers either sit facing or stand depending on what is being said to an employee. Can you think of other examples?

DAY 23
COURAGE

Reading in Matthew 14:22-33 this morning was more encouragement for what I fix my gaze upon.

This is the story of Jesus walking on the water. The disciples were in the boat, no land in sight, and big waves were pounding them. Rocking back and forth fear arose in them that the boat might capsize. It was the middle of the night, dark, and terrifying. But they see a figure on the water coming toward them. They thought it was a ghost. Jesus speaks and tells them to not be afraid. He tells them to take courage.

Peter speaks and asks if it is He, then to beckon him come to Him on the water. Jesus invites him and Peter quickly gets out of the boat and begins walking toward Jesus — ON THE WATER! Then you know what happens.

But Peter takes his eyes off Jesus, looks at the strong winds making the huge waves and immediately starts to sink. Terrified and sinking, Jesus reaches out to take his hand and save him. He asks Peter why he doubted. Once back in the boat with Jesus the winds were calm and they made it safely to shore.

Is this true for any of you? I've been there more times than I want to recall. It is the middle of the night, the house is asleep and you are awake. Are you sick? Are you worried? Did you hear something and it caused you concern? Your brain won't shut off so you can enter slumber? Or maybe it is not the middle of the night but during the day and something happens. I am sure we all have stories of being afraid. Fear comes out of nowhere.

Lord, it is assuring to know that when you ask us to "fear not" you are saying, "trust me." Help us each time we get anxious. Help us to view the thing, condition, circumstance with your eyes and give it over to you, calling on your name. The one name above all names, which brings the answer, solution and restores peace in us. Amen.

When was the last time you were afraid, fearful, or anxious about something? Did you lose sleep? Did you feel sick to your stomach? Did your minutes or hours of worry gain anything of value to you? How long did it take to restore you to peace? Like I said, I have been there more often than I wish.

I mentioned I grew up in a dysfunctional home. I have several traits ingrained in me from both of my parents. Some traits are good but most, not so good. Sometimes when I mention them to others, people can't understand because their upbringing was different. Their paradigm and experiences are learned in an entirely different way. What is one person's Achilles heel is not another person's.

I had a long season in life when I struggled with being a hypochondriac. I have suffered all of my life as far back as I can recall. My mother was the model/poster child for this disorder. As much as I didn't like it growing up I found myself falling prey to it as an adult. I pray, I trust, I rely on Jesus and yet it rears its ugly head every time I get any pain. I think the worst; envision peril time after time after time.

Every time I say "I'm not going to do this anymore. Today is the day I am a different person. I am full of faith. The Lord is in control and I will not fear…" I fail before the day is out. Exhausting!

I wish I could say, "Here are the skills I've used successfully to get victory in this area." All I can say is that now I find myself feeling less peril and instead more peace. I've tried to dig deep into the Lord, recite his Word and believe. Then we had a global pandemic this year and I found myself dreading the virus at every turn. So I inquired of the Lord as to the root cause. Was there more than my hypochondriac condition to deal with to gain freedom? I think for me, the root fear is dying. Although I know it is inevitable for every human I am just not keen on dying until we all go to meet Jesus. I don't want to leave people I love behind. I want the maximum time with them I can get.

Even though I trust Jesus and know I have a home in heaven for eternity I want to stay here on earth as long as I can. Just being real with you. I know there are others, like me, who suffer with this foreboding dilemma and many suffer in silence. Even though I have tons of family and friends already in heaven I think since it isn't a place I can tangibly see I struggle at changing addresses.

The whispering I hear today is *courage* which is defined as the ability to do something that frightens one; strength in the face of pain or grief. I need more courage!

Do you have an area in your life where you struggle and like Paul in the Bible you wish to do those things you don't and instead do those things you wish you didn't? It is human. It makes us able to relate to our fellow humans.

How do you give hope to others in the area of your fear/anxiety? Can you work at it like me, asking the Lord for a daily dose of courage?

that still small *Whisper*

DAY 24
MERCY

This morning I flipped to a small letter written from Jude who was the brother of James. We might like to refer to his letter as a memo since it is only one chapter and twenty-five verses. The summation of his letter was warning fellow believers to be careful of those claiming faith and salvation but who are actually not part of the body of Christ.

Even long ago there were those who came to the church and remained only to cause division. They were skeptics and eager to pick apart believers for their faith. They grumbled and complained. Nothing suited them. They lied and held to their natural instincts because the Spirit was not in them. They defied authority. They were boasting, in verse four of God's wonderful, compassionate, all covering grace that would allow them to lead immoral lives. They hated what they didn't understand.

Jude is encouraging the faithful in verse twenty-two to show mercy to those whose faith may be wavering, on the fence, teetering, could easily fall away due to the convincing claims of the misguided. He ends the letter with all the glory given to Jesus, the Christ, who is able to keep them and bring them with joy one day to His glorious presence. It is His majesty, power, greatness, and authority which was in the beginning before time, pervasively now and forever in eternity.

Lord, help us to recognize and not be swayed by those who claim to be followers of Christ but lack the Spirit within them. May we strengthen our fellow Christians when we see them being lead astray by what they are hearing which is not the life and light of Your Word. Amen.

I hear the whispering of *mercy* today. Just as I am so blessed by the grace that God provides freely to us, I am equally happy for His mercy. Mercy is compassion or forgiveness shown toward someone whom it is within one's power to punish. Where would we be without mercy?

In the letter Jude writes God could easily handle the misguided, ill-informed divisors among them. He chose not to, instead calling the early young believers to watch for and show mercy to those who could be victims.

The Bible is full of examples where God was merciful and yet the person receiving did exactly the opposite. Think about the man who had a huge debt the Lord forgave. Instead of showing that same mercy and forgiveness to one in debt to him he immediately went out and demanded repayment from the debtor. Wow!

Can you think of a time when the Lord showed you mercy when you yourself would not have extended it to another?

I grew up in a strict home, not a lot of mercy there. If you did something wrong, you were severely punished. Like the saying goes, "for the crime, do the time." In my case I was punished for "crimes" I didn't commit. There was no escape or being let off the hook. My parents explained that the punishing was so that I would never even be "tempted" to do x, y, or z infraction. As a tiny child I had no clue what this meant. All I understood was spankings could come out of nowhere and at any time.

As I got older, I learned to expect them anytime and anywhere. My parents explained it as their way of loving me and it was because they cared how I turned out. This was the method my parents used to reinforce the rules and to hopefully drive home the point to be obedient.

When I did have a lapse in judgment and made a mistake, it was my parent's responsibility to pick the punishment befitting the offense or disobedience.

I was not a fan of the home rules when I was a kid, but I was obedient and managed to comply. I am thankful for those rules and boundaries. They kept me from falling prey to the persuasive voices of peers, the ones who could have led me away from the right way of living.

I so often wished my parents had shown me love in the form of hugs, affirming words and taking pride in their child. It was only well into my adult life that I was able to look back and understand them from their own childhoods. Those emotions and tangible forms of affection were non-existent for them. They had never seen it modeled or experienced it, they were parenting as they had been parented. Though I can't excuse or condone their behavior, I understand. But the pattern had to stop. I wanted my family to know I loved them.

Are you excited and thrilled that our heavenly parent is full of mercy? Think of all the things we do every day that could easily evoke a response and yet He is slow to wrath and anger. He decides when and what punishment is warranted, if any. Praise God!

Have you ever "got off easy" compared to what could have happened for "x, y, and z?" Who held the mercy in that case? Keep a prayerful watch over those who could be easily enticed into worldly living that doesn't feed or align their soul with the Spirit of God.

that still small **Whisper**

DAY 25
LOVE

I turned to Mark and thought I'd share some scripture on wellness/wholeness for our body, which is the temple where the Holy Spirit resides. Chapter 1:40-45 (NIV) tells the story of Jesus healing a man with leprosy.

I don't know about you, but I am hearing people each day talking about one area of weakness or another. It could be emotional or physical or both. It is true that as long as we live in this earthly home our bodies will have issues. We are mortal in frame AND house the Holy Spirit in our inmost parts. It only stands to reason, like my husband has always said, "when you are sick you must do the natural and the spiritual." I like to pray and proclaim that my body would come in alignment to the Word of God!

Like the man in the biblical account he came and humbled himself, kneeling before Jesus and begged to be healed. He understood and was mentally assured Jesus could do as requested. It says Jesus was "moved with compassion," He reached out and touched him and made the declaration "Be healed!" Instantly, the leprosy disappeared.

After this Jesus sent the man away with a stern warning. Don't tell anyone and instead go to the priest (so he can see your healed state), make the offering required in the Law of Moses. *This will be a public testimony*. Verse forty-five begins with, "Instead he went out and began to talk freely, spreading the news…" As a result, Jesus had large crowds flocking to him wherever He went, making it harder to approach him individually. I wonder about the man. The leprosy disappeared instantly but was the healing COMPLETE? Could he have had an outward manifestation awaiting the competed inward work?

We know God heals today through natural means, medical intervention, and miracles. People often wonder why they aren't healed if they believe and have faith. Many ask, "Am I not showing faith in God for a miracle if I seek out medical intervention?" I know several that will not take prescription medication because they prefer and only want to use "natural" methods. The list goes on and on. I am sure you each know people who tackle the wellness of their bodies in less than conventional medical methods. Why God chooses to heal one way or another is still a mystery.

I look back at the story for some keys, principles and actions the Lord is whispering to me. I hear *love*.

First: Taking a posture of humbleness before the Lord when requesting of Him.

Second: Stating, "if you are willing" (not if it is Your will - people misquote this a lot.)

Third: Request and make your desire known.

When Jesus took action, He addressed these three things. Jesus was moved out of pure *love*, which is the whispering for today. His divinity was moved with human compassion. From a humbled posture Jesus touched with His willingness. There was no need to reach, just receive; fully persuaded and convinced Jesus could meet any request asked of Him.

Lord, thank you for your love. May I always be found postured in reverence to receive your touches in my life. I am glad you hear my heartfelt requests. Continue to help me grow in confidence of your miraculous power in me through the Spirit. Amen.

With God's love totally enveloping our being, we can understand His nature to move with compassion in our lives. How can we, His hands and feet, extend that love to others with hearts full of compassion and make a difference? Can you think of a person who could use a healthy dose of love from you today? Could God be asking to use you as His extended healing reach? Might He want to use you to vocally command, "Be Healed" through His powerful Spirit in you? Have you been in a position or recall a time you were able to help someone with a blessing only God could have done through you?

that still small Whisper

DAY 26

FAMILY

This morning I read 3 John. This is a very short letter with a single theme. This was an encouragement letter celebrating how hospitable Gaius had been to the traveling teachers (missionaries). I think of the wonderful people around the world who give up their homes, to go and live in foreign lands, sharing the Word of the Lord.

Imagine how it would feel to arrive at a new town or village where someone took you into their home and treated you warmly. This letter also has the flip side beginning in verse nine with details about those who don't welcome with warmth and care.

Lord, may we be as mindful today as then about how we welcome and treat the people who make it their lives work to spread the Good News. May we be generous and gracious toward them. Amen.

I am sure you each know of missionaries who have traveled abroad. They heard God calling them to go and share Christ and his message. Many of these people have given up so much to follow that call. We have even been treated to reports when they come home of the wonderful things happening with the Gospel. It is very exciting.

Today the whispering I hear is the word *family*. We all have an inclusive unit by blood and with the acceptance of Christ we also have brothers and sisters with whom we share a heavenly Father. My extended spiritual family intrigues me because they are of all nationalities and live all over the globe.

I have two very dear friends. One I have known since Sunday School days and going to public school together. When I did attend church, she was always there as her parents were very active and her aunt and uncle were missionaries. My friend married the choir director at our church. After she and her husband had their family, they decided to become missionaries. They now serve as pastors for an International Church in Florence, Italy.

We have kept in touch and periodically I would send offerings to help with their budget. A few years back I got an email from them stating a native Italian couple who were active in their congregation were traveling to the states. They asked if I would I be able to help them get to east Texas where they were scheduled to be helping hands at a Christian retreat center for two weeks. My husband and I gladly said yes and even mentioned we would drive them to the camp and go back and get them two weeks later.

We met Giovanni and Gina when they landed and became fast and great friends. They are two of the most kind and compassionate people I have ever met. We had the blessing of being able to host them in our home before and after their trip to the camp. I loved hearing their excitement for the Gospel. It was infectious and exhilarating!

We traveled the few hours by car sharing what we could with our lack of mastery of the others native tongue. We were so happy for them to be headed on this adventure. They had never served outside of Italy before and were "pumped" to serve the Lord at the camp.

We arrived at the camp. It was August. August in Texas is HOT! When we got out of our car, I was expecting the people who ran the camp to throw open the welcome doors. To my shock, they were not excited to have our visitors from Italy there as help for two weeks. Apparently, there had been a miscommunication and the staff of the camp didn't know what to do with Giovanni and Gina.

Our new Italian family mentioned they had traveled a long distance and had nowhere else to go for two weeks. They would do whatever the camp needed; clean, cook, and make beds. They just wanted to serve, the whole purpose for their trip. After a few very anxious moments the camp staff agreed they could use them and house them.

My husband and I left feeling very uncomfortable about dropping off our "new" family where they had been less than warmly received. We conversed about it all the way home. How could a Christian camp staff treat fellow Christians this way? Would they be okay? Should we go back and get them and bring them to our home?

When we returned two weeks later to gather them and bring them back to our home we found they had developed a few good friends among the staff, although there were still some who were less than cordial. Giovanni and Gina did not want to focus on the negatives, instead they wanted to share the wonderful touching stories they had from the kids they met who were campers and how they felt honored to have served.

I did push a bit to find out the whole story. Seems they were not housed in one of the staff cabins but instead sent to a resource trailer, with no air conditioning! Yes, sent to live in a HOT metal tube of a home. They put them to work cleaning, with very little interaction with the attendees of the camp. Hardly the huge serving experience they had planned and been so excited about when they left Italy. The story was horrid, but this couple had huge smiles, they never complained and were instead grateful to have served.

They spent a few days in our home before returning to Italy. We took them sightseeing and even enjoyed a time of fellowship with our home group as they brought us the lesson. We enjoyed them so very much and were so grateful God gave us time to bond.

Since then we have hosted them again and they even made a trip to Arizona to serve at a camp there. This is what they do with their vacation, come to America and serve.

While in Arizona, I made arrangements for them to meet my daughter and her extended family that live in a suburb of Phoenix. My daughter sent us pictures of them going out to eat. Now my blood family are friends with Giovanni and Gina. The cool thing is when my husband can physically travel and it is feasible we are going to visit our missionary friends in Florence and we will also visit Giovanni and Gina. This is how the international family of God grows.

How about you? I know there are many of you who have extended people around the globe who are friends and fellow brothers and sisters in Christ. Have you been to see them in their home country? How was the hospitality compared to what you were expecting? If they are serving with the Gospel what are they doing? I think we will see our "whispering family" has extended family everywhere!

DAY 27
GROW

Today as I was reading in 2 Corinthians 13 I thought I'd skip to the end of Paul's letter and see how he signed off. Verse eleven states, "...I close my letter with these words: Be joyful. Grow to maturity. Encourage each other. Live in harmony and peace. Then the God of love and peace will be with you." (NLT) Another translation says, "...keep rejoicing and repair whatever is broken..." (VOICE) The words are a pretty good summation of how to live. It certainly goes to show the same is true today as then.

Lord, help us to take the directives of Paul and apply them to our daily life. We are grateful for the opportunity to be Christian examples of love, peace and maturity. Amen.

The whispering I hear today is *grow*. When we are growing, we are becoming. We can change. When we apply the maturity of living, which comes with growth, we can expand the level of our joy, love, and peace. Doing it with one another is encouraging. Helping one another repair brokenness is hard but a lot can happen when we come alongside someone who is struggling.

Can you imagine a world of harmony and peace? A Coke commercial from 1971 began like this..."I'd like to teach the world to sing in perfect harmony..." The idea is not new but the hunger for a world at peace will always be worth our effort to attain.

that
still *whisper*
small

DAY 28
TRUTH

I read the very short letter, 2 John, written to a "lady and her children" referring to the Church and its members. The central idea here is love and truth. John is encouraging them in how to live with the command God gave to love one another. To also be mindful of those who are deceiving the body of Christ — not having any truth in them.

Today's whispering is *truth*. There were then, just as there are now, many who deny that God came in a bodily form. They plant seeds of doubt, enough to convince many, to leave the faith and to turn from the commandment to love.

Lord, we honor your Lordship in our life and in the world. We want to always be found standing firm in our belief of who you were when you walked the earth and who you continue to be on Your throne and in our hearts. Amen.

Truth defined is a fact, belief or reality accepted as true. This letter from John talked about truth in God's love as a "measurable action not a sentimental emotion." I think a challenge we have as believers is to dose out love to those around us. We achieve that in the measure we are convinced and secure is the absolute truth. Like your personal testimony, it is truth because you have lived it. You are not just telling a story you heard or something someone shared with you about someone else. This is why the Lord told us to love and to share <u>our own</u> testimony.

I think if we could each spend part of our quiet time reflecting on what God has done for us, specifically, and ask Him where and who to share this truth with, in love, we may be surprised with the outcome in lives of those we come in contact.

DAY 29
WITNESS

3 John was written to a friend and encourages Gaius in the hospitality he offered to missionaries. 2 John was written to "the lady and her children," the church and its members, focusing on love and truth. Today I read 1 John which was written to a community of churches comprised mostly of non-Jews. As a gentle parent he testifies to them from his own personal experience, like we mentioned yesterday in regard to truth.

Look at how John, proclaimed to be the disciple most loved by Jesus, starts this letter. Verse one is speaking of *them* referencing he and the other disciples. "…We have seen him with our own eyes, heard him with our own ears, and touched him with our own hands…" (VOICE) WOW! Can you imagine, just for a moment, having someone encourage you with his or her own *testimony* of hearing, seeing and touching JESUS! The disciples walked and talked with Him every day. They shared community together. Eternal life in the flesh, *with* them.

We know the power we can engage toward others is when we share our own experiences, things we have negotiated, successes we have had, and hardships we have overcome. There is power in what we know to be true because we have lived it, journeyed that road and walked in those shoes. When you share with someone, about *how* God has touched your life there is power, life-giving light goes forth from you to others. They may not have had an experience of their own (yet).

Lord, we accept your Word, written in the Bible from so many who knew you, as absolute truth. May the Word come alive every time we open the Bible. As our eyes scan the words may they sink into our Spirit and witness there of your majesty, mercy, grace and LOVE. Help us to radiate it all around us. Amen.

The whispering I hear today is *witness*. This is defined as a person who sees an event and provides evidence and proof. Just like one can be called in to court to give testimony about an event, accident, crime or happening. The judge and court want to hear first-hand accounts of what was seen, heard and experienced.

If we are witnesses for God and how He has touched us, it carries authentic and reliable evidence for who He is and what He has done. Far too many people have experienced His life giving attributes for it to be false or contrived. May each of us take a few minutes to reflect on our own life and remember what He has done. Take a moment to write a list.

Once you have your list of all He has done, imagine what He is doing behind the scenes now, which will soon be discovered by you and added to your testimony. Every morning is another day to have an experience to add to our own testimony.

Some of you may be thinking, "What do we do with the bad experiences that don't seem life giving or pleasurable? How do we use them to witness to others?" You may be dealing with something and not sure of the outcome and wonder how anyone could be encouraged if you shared that story.

Sometimes the very hardest and most difficult time to sing praises to the King and worship His awesome might and power is when you are struggling. It might be physical, financial, or relationship oriented. The Bible tells us though we are to be thankful and praise in <u>all circumstanc-</u>

es. But it can be harder in difficult situations, and goes contrary to our emotions, at the moment. Sometimes we do all we can to just hang on. The anguish can be unbearable.

Shortly before Ken and I married, something horrible happened when my husband came home for lunch, as he does most days. When he pulled into the driveway he noticed the back door was smashed in and the window broken.

He had two children living at home, had recently given temporary shelter to a third person who was a friend of one of his children. He ventured inside, which he later admits wasn't too smart if an intruder had still been present, to find broken tile flooring in his kitchen and items missing from his living room. His closet was disheveled and his safe was missing. In the safe were personal documents and financial information useful enough to prove identity. The thief had enough information to steal Ken's identity and go on a spending spree. And the thief had wasted no time setting up accounts and charging things.

Ken spent the better part of months going from police station to police station, store to store filling out criminal reports, and calling all the credit reporting agencies. It was exhausting. Big items like the TV and gaming station could be replaced, but it was expensive. The personal family documents and heirloom items in the safe could never be replaced. The violation he felt personally was overwhelming.

No one knew who had done it even though the third party, who had lived in his home but had not been present for a month, seemed suspect. The police said in many cases the perpetrators are never found. The missing checks, temporary driver's license, and social security card used to build an ID were still out there. It was like being violated and then waiting for the violation to happen again and again.

He prayed and walked this out each day. I asked Ken if he had thanked the Lord that the intruder was not there when he walked in the door that afternoon, thankful no one was hurt in the theft. He could have been injured or killed. His children were not home and they had been spared. I had not come over to cook an early dinner for him and the kids or else I could have been a target myself. His house had not been burned to the ground causing his family to lose everything. He hadn't thanked the Lord yet.

I mentioned to him about praying like it says in Philippians 4:6, "don't worry about anything; instead, pray about everything. Tell God what you need and thank him for all he has done." (NLT) Then, peace will come. The key principles I felt were:

- Not to WORRY
- Pray about it ALL
- Tell God what you NEED
- THANK Him for ALL
- PEACE will reign

We did exactly this. Ken spent an entire day devoted to thanksgiving to the Lord. The next day, a call came from the police station asking Ken to come in as they had something for him. Seems the day before a driver witnessed an altercation with two men on the street. When one of the men broke away and ran off, he dropped something. The driver got out to retrieve the item, calling police and giving the account of what he saw. The item dropped was a wallet with everything used to build Ken's fake ID. They now were back in Ken's possession and peace came to Ken.

Some might call it a coincidence, but Ken and I know for a fact the hand of God spun the situation based on prayer. Being thankful instead of fearful. Praying for divine intervention. Being firm in our positive hope instead of negative. Telling God what we needed and releasing the outcome to him to control.

What is there you might be struggling with in which you might appropriate a prayer of thanksgiving to the Lord? When your mind and emotions are screaming NO could you turn the table and tell the Lord you are thankful for ALL he has done and is doing for you, sight unseen? The results, though they may not be immediate as in my story, will profit you immensely!

that still small *whisper*

DAY 30
HEIRS

This morning I was reading in Galatians 3 and 4. This is where Paul is speaking about the law and promise made by God. In 3:16 he is careful to point out God's promises were given to Abraham and his *child*, not children. Chapter 3:17 talks about the agreement made and how God could not break his promise, when he gave Moses the Law over four hundred years later. Chapter 3:18 shows us the promise of God is our inheritance. The promise, the child, is Jesus Christ.

Paul goes on to explain why the law was given — to keep people's sin in check until the child (the promised one) arrived whom would carry the freedom from sin when He, was accepted by people. Chapter 3:24 sums it up nicely. The "...law was our guardian; until Christ came and protected us until we could be made right with God through faith." (NLT) Chapter 3:29 states as believers we are true children of Abraham and heirs to God's promise. And it belongs to us!

If you read on in chapter four it explains further. The good news is, we who believe are *heirs*, the whispering for today. We can enjoy the blessings spoken about long ago.

Lord, as the seed of promise spoken so long ago, I want to thank you for entrusting your nature to us via the Holy Spirit. May we listen each day to what the Spirit speaks and walk in the freedom you provided, not weighed down by sin. Thank you for the work on the cross that gave new life to all. Amen.

"Heir" means a person legally entitled to the property and continuing the legacy of a predecessor. Being an heir of God through Christ and empowered by the Holy Spirit is a tremendous blessing and responsibility. I think of someone who lives a meager life and then a wealthy person dies leaving their unimaginable inheritance to them. Suddenly they are wealthy beyond what they could have ever thought possible. What do they do? What would *you* do?

We are that person, dead and poor in our sinful nature and lifestyle. Then we accept Christ and become wealthier than we could have ever dreamed. We have available to us untold riches of the kingdom. It is at our disposal to use as the Holy Spirit directs us. Be honest, in the example above talking about inheritance did you immediately think money? In human reasoning that is where most people's mind goes, to the tangible evidence of wealth.

For a moment, think in terms of wealth in the Spirit sense. How many of you have lost older family members, teachers, mentors, and/or guardians who left you with riches of their wisdom, their character, and the way they lived? They may or may not have had money (which is here today and gone tomorrow and isn't making the trip home with us anyway). What they did impart to you was given freely because you had the good fortune to have known them and be touched by them in your lifetime.

Think of a few of these precious people and what you gained from them that is with you today. Who were they? What did they leave that you value enough to hopefully give away as an inheritance one day? I think we will all see how rich we are and blessed beyond our wildest dreams.

My great aunt was like a grandmother to me because she lived close and my grandma lived in California. This aunt was the spiritual pillar in our family. I learned to cook from her and when I needed prayer, she was the go to person. She could reach the Lord and you could *feel* it.

As a young girl she attended Sunday school in southern California and her teacher was Amiee Simple McPherson. Amiee was a pillar of faith and a Holy Roller in her time before the term became Pentecostal fashionable. What a legacy to have had this person teaching you in the ways of God.

It was this aunt who I went to the day I felt a strange tugging at my heart I'd never experienced before. She recognized it as God's wooing and took me to a revival (just happened to be going on at our family church that week). I was positioned to receive my heavenly inheritance. That night, my salvation experience, will forever be etched in my heart.

When I accepted Christ and committed to live anew, shedding my poor sinful life for hope, peace, and unconditional love it was indeed better than winning the lottery. I didn't obtain worldly wealth but what I gained in my Spirit was far superior to an elevated bank account. What I had to *spend at my disposal* was a never ending, bottomless, and overflowing account of love.

That night changed me. Though I have had times where life has caused me turmoil and pain, I know deep inside who's child I am and what I have in my heart that can never be taken away.

When my dear aunt passed, I got some tangible items I inherited, they make me think of her even today. The most precious of them are her bible studies from the early 1900s. Though very worn and the paper fragile, I can see her handwritten notes as she learned about Jesus. Can't put a price on that. I study the Word every chance I can and sometimes it is fun to look and read through these antique treasures.

Since the night of my salvation, I have written morsels of goodness I gain though whispers in my heart. I love teaching others where God has given me a *rhema word*. I write them in the white pages of my Bible. As one Bible gets "too busy" with my notes, I purchase another and write more. To date I have four Bibles with white space nuggets. I intend to pass them to my grandchildren. I hope they will be a legacy to each of them like what my aunt passed to me. It is my hope and prayer the young ones will reflect on what is there and one day leave this tangible token to their grandchildren.

I am my aunt's heir and continuing her legacy is a daunting task. Humbly, I submit to continue sowing into others — the richest blessing I've known since I asked Jesus into my heart.

(Note: These next few entries were written during the Christmas season. Some don't have a scripture reference. Enjoy them on whatever days you happen to be reading.)

DAY 31
GIVE

I don't have a passage of scripture today. I was reading through many chapters and listening to the whisperings of living the life God meant for us to live. We have examples from the writings of Paul, Peter, John, and more with examples on how to live like Christ. It is all there for us to read, absorb, and apply to our life.

I want to encourage you in the here and now, in this season of life and in our present circumstances. I sense it is more about "feeling" with one another, those things that seem to burden us to the point of where our joy and hope is zapped.

In the hurry up lifestyle of our culture, most people are so weighed down instead of feeling free and lighthearted. It is especially true at the holidays, like Christmas. For some reason we have taken the joy of a day meant to celebrate a promised child's birth and made it so commercial and expensive. True meaning gets lost among the torn and tossed wrapping paper and colorful bows.

Lord, as a festive season is upon us may each person unwrap your nature. Amen.

I'm going to offer my whispering today, *give*, as gifts to unwrap. I won't attach a nametag because I know God will shine a bright light on the whisper for you. In many cases I am sure you can unwrap multiple packages of whispers here. Take as few or as many gifts as you like.

In package one I hear CARE — take care of yourself first and then assist those around you.

In package two I hear PEACE — take more than a few moments to breathe. Focus more on what peace feels like circulating through your entire being.

In package three I hear HARMONY — what it really means to you when people cooperate with each other for the benefit of community.

In package four I hear NURTURE — not that you need to do it for others as much as you need to receive it from someone who continually is offering it to you.

In package five I hear GROWTH — and not in the physical sense instead in the spiritual sense. God is using the days in the immediate future to grow you in ways you will find beneficial for something you have wanted and asked about over time. If it seems difficult at first, like putting on new jeans, go ahead because what He is doing is custom made for you.

In package six I hear RETREAT — not going backwards like away from a battle but instead going away with the Lord. I sense there are a few of you who would be surprised by taking a retreat with the Lord. He has something very important to tell you and He needs you away where you can hear and be expecting only Him.

In package seven I see something and it is a CHILD — I don't get the feeling anyone is expecting as much as someone needs to become more childlike. There are things God wants to give you, but it has to be taken in the way a child would with utter joy and no strings attached.

In package eight I felt POWER — it was an amazing thing to behold. It carried such strength and His authority but tendered with kindness.

In package nine I felt BOLDNESS — as there are a few of you who have been asking for more boldness in not only your personal life but your work life too. He wants you to not only take hold of it but step into it.

In package ten I saw a FLOWER in its bud form — not yet fully opened. It gives me pause, there are many of you still gently wrapped in the pedals of all God has for you. It is time for you to push the pedals forward into others' lives and as you do there will come a fragrance. God is waiting to smell the perfume of your life as you reach out.

In the last package I see a pair of SHOES — and these are not pretty shoes as much as they are worn and have no soles on them. Tucked in the corner is a small round mirror. At first it was difficult to see those worn out shoes but when I reached for the mirror I realized it wasn't to be used to gaze at a face as much as used to look at the soles of the feet. The feet were worn from years of use. The Lord clearly impressed to me that when He sees calloused feet He sees VICTORY. He sees someone who is going the distance and is about to reap from an area they have long been praying about. There is something you have toiled over, pleaded, and shed tears over which is going to be answered.

I would be elated to open and claim any of these packages. I trust God will shine His light on your gift or gifts.

I am sensing some people may say that none of these are yours. I was crying because God heard it too. The thing I felt in my heart is not only is one gift for you, but they are ALL for you. Take them as yours and know a huge God desires more for you than you are imagining for yourself. He is the gift giver.

that still small **Whisper**

DAY 32
QUIET

We can get busy. From the time our feet hit the floor we are on the move, rarely set aside moments for absolute quiet, uninterrupted tranquil time with the Lord.

Today I am offering my day to you, my readers. What are your needs and concerns?

I want to take time and just pray that the Lord would touch every hand that holds this devotional.

Lord, I am committing this day for my friends and the concerns they have. I am waiting on a whisper for them specifically, to bring light into whatever situation they seek. Amen.

I love each of you and the whisper for today is *quiet*. Shhh… listen to the blissful sound of nothing. Be the best version of YOU, never stressed and always blessed.

that still small *Whisper*

DAY 33
GIFT

I was drawn to think about Mary, the mother of Jesus and how she must have felt getting close to the delivery of her child. I had my first child the day after Christmas and know what it felt like to be *very* pregnant leading up to the holidays. In the days of Mary and Joseph they weren't awaiting Santa, holiday shopping or gifting presents but instead were traveling. I can only imagine the thoughts going through both of them, as the baby was due to arrive.

Lord, I am very thankful for the gift of your holiness born into this world as a flesh and blood human, able to feel and experience the things common to us all. Without Jesus, where would we be today? Amen.

The whisper I am hearing is *gift*. Christ, as a baby, was born and became for many the greatest gift one could ever receive. He is the gift that keeps giving into our life. We learned from those who knew him personally when we read bible stories. We still receive intimate knowledge from the Holy Spirit whom God left with us to guide and enlighten us every day. It just doesn't get better than that.

that still small **Whisper**

DAY 34
PEACE

'Twas the day before Christmas, as I read and pray,

In the quietness to ponder, what God has to say?

The silence is peace, and His comfort is love,

Granting me the treasure, I seek from above.

Today is the mad shopping day for all the procrastinators, the time to get to the store and gather those last minute items for holiday food and gift giving. It is also a time to begin the day with prayer and to seek wisdom from the Lord.

Today I was reading in Mark 6 and circulating in my heart was the whisper *peace*. It means free from disturbance; quiet, calm.

It seems everywhere Jesus went he moved about rather calmly. Others around him might be excited, act nervously, and get anxious but Jesus was calm. Like we have read before and in this passage — the story is about Jesus walking on the water.

In verse forty-five Jesus insists the disciples get in their boat <u>immediately</u> after the miracle feeding of the five thousand so they can get to the other side of the lake. Verse forty-eight, <u>late that night</u> Jesus notices the disciples (in the middle of the lake) are in serious trouble. About three in the morning He came toward them walking on the water. <u>He intended to go past them</u>. Verse forty-nine is when the disciples saw Him, scripture says they cried, were *terrified* thinking they were seeing a ghost. Jesus speaks "Don't be afraid, Take courage! I am here!" (NLT) Then Jesus climbed in the boat and the wind stopped. They were amazed, shocked, and thrilled. CALM and PEACE was physically amongst them. Peace is a person, not a feeling. Peace is Jesus.

The other gospel accounts of this story are about the same except Matthew mentions Peter asking to come to the Lord on the water. Mark mentions that Jesus got in the boat. Luke doesn't even mention the story. It makes me wonder why the disciples in the boat relate the story differently. Why the statement about the miracle of the loaves on the heels of the terrifying boat ordeal? It was as if once the horrific and exhausting moment in the storm was over, they could relax and go back to what they were thinking about before peril came upon them.

Miracles don't make you have faith. Sometimes it can do the opposite. You have faith and then see the signs (miracles). The disciples, much like us, when in doubt about the nature of Jesus and God working, will always be wondering and need to be convinced. This will inhibit a growth in faith. It finally took the disciples witnessing the resurrection to be convinced. What will it take for us? Do you have a story about an event that locked in the dial on your faith?

Lord, may we take peace and comfort from the fact you are near to us at *all times*. When the winds of life blow on us we will not be terrified but exude calm, trusting peace which is only found in you through the Holy Spirit — our great comforter. Amen.

What storm are you rowing in right now, terrified and crying out to stop? Look for Jesus around you and invite him into your boat to speak BE STILL and let His serene presence invade and overtake you.

DAY 35
JESUS

My reading today is from Matthew and Luke, giving the account of the birth of Jesus.

In Matthew 1:20-21 (NLT) the Angel said to Joseph, <u>as he appeared to him in a dream,</u> "…Joseph, son of David, do not be afraid to take Mary as your wife. For the child within her was conceived by the Holy Spirit. And she will have a son, and you are to name him Jesus, for he will save his people from their sins."

Luke 1:28-38 (NLT) tells us what the Angel (Gabriel) said to Mary. He said, "…Greetings, favored woman! The Lord is with you!" This confused and disturbed Mary, as she didn't know what the Angel meant. "Don't be afraid, Mary, for you have found favor with God! You will conceive and give birth to a son, and you will call him Jesus. He will be very great and will be called Son of the Most High. The Lord will give him the throne of his ancestor David. He will reign over Israel forever; his kingdom will never end!"

Mary asks how this will happen; she is a virgin. The Angel responded, "The Holy Spirit will come upon you, and the power of the Most High will overshadow you. So the baby to be born will be holy, and he will be called the Son of God." The Angel goes on to tell her of the miracle with her cousin Elizabeth and demonstrates nothing is impossible with God.

Mary responds with, "I am the Lord's servant. May everything you have said about me come true."

Seems only right to me that the Angel would give more details to Mary as she is about to carry and birth the Christ child. Joseph just needed the facts, taking her as his wife. The Angel came to Joseph in a <u>dream, talking</u>. The Angel came to Mary, <u>appearing in front of her, to speak.</u>

I try to imagine being in Mary's shoes and the great promise to carry within you God's own son for nine months. Then the time came for her to deliver.

Lord, I take from this passage the power of believing when heaven speaks. I want to tune my ear to hear and obey as direction comes from your throne. Amen.

The whisper for today is *Jesus*. There is no name more powerful, wonderful, and majestic in the world. Rejoice every day, sometime in your day, remembering the King of Kings was born for **us**!

DAY 36
VICTORY

My Bible reading today is from Hebrews 4:14-16. It talks about Jesus entering Heaven, having died and then raised to new life in God. How do we hold firm to what we have come to believe?

I like how verse fifteen states that Jesus understands our weaknesses because he faced all the same testing we do. He was human with everyday trials. The exception is He did not sin. He met the challenge and reacted as an example for how God would respond, without sinning.

Verse sixteen promises if we boldly, on purpose, with deliberation and not being shy or meek come to the throne of God, we <u>will</u> receive *mercy* and we <u>will</u> receive *grace*. These two components of Gods nature are needed by us to claim victory.

In our times of struggle when it would be easy to sin, running to Jesus will provide us what we need. Jesus is our mediator. He is the very extension of God and also the sacrifice to cover our sin. He provides mercy and grace.

Jesus called all of us to be Priests to each other. There will be times when you will be the hands and feet, nourishing and praying with someone in need. Your kindness and attention show mercy and grace as a reflection of Christ living in you. Sins we commit and the pain we suffer from situations and circumstances will require us to receive mercy and grace. Can you give to others and be willing to let another mortal human bear your burden with you to the throne? Do you feel you must shoulder your sin yourself? It doesn't work that way. We need others to be for us what we are to them.

Lord, help us to see those opportunities when you are positioning others to be a cup of refreshing water, a shoulder to weep on and a voice to proclaim to the heavens our desire for mercy and grace. Thank you that by giving and receiving we are patterning after you and will find victory and peace. Amen.

The whisper today is *victory*. This is an act of defeating an enemy or opponent. Triumph and conquest are synonymous terms. The peace we gain from being victorious over situations where the enemy would like to trap us or bind us can only be found when we accept the mercy and grace Jesus brought us from God. Because He is in us, we have access to this provision when we extend to others and let them extend to us.

When I think of the victories I've attained in life I'm pleased with how the Lord brought me through so many things. Yet, I still have struggles where victory is a bit out of reach. I am always on the lookout for where the victory will come and who will be there to help me along the way.

The story I am about to share is powerful, especially if you identify with the problem — being overweight and lacking exercise. Now don't run away, this story will bring you, like it did me, a way to victory. This is from my son-in-law, Brandon.

My daughter, Christina married her husband Brandon the same year I married Ken. In the past twenty years we have all lived in Texas (except for a brief time when they lived in Georgia) but we've never lived in the same city. After my daughter had her two children I wanted to spend as much time as I could near them so I could spoil the little ones. We pick the story up in 2010 when my grandchildren were ten and five.

I had gotten worried about Brandon and Christina because they were both suffering from being overweight. (I had no room to talk, as I have been forty to fifty pounds past my desired weight for years.) I didn't want them to have to suffer the many things that come from carrying too much weight when they were still young.

Brandon's wellness journey started with a trip to the doctor for a general physical and blood work. As a child, he had suffered being overweight. Later he had a time when he yo-yoed up and down the scale, sometimes losing too much and almost being anorexic and then back higher than his ideal weight. The lifelong battle to attain proper weight always seemed to loom over him. His world was about to take a dramatic turn.

The doctor told him his blood level triglycerides were in the 700s, normal is under 150 mg/dl. Since they use them to factor a formula for determining low density lipids (LDL) the doctor told Brandon the formula couldn't be run. In essence his next step would be to choose a coffin if he didn't get serious about achieving a normal body mass index. (I will interject here. Scales will never tell you your health because so many factors need to be considered. If you are a scale watcher, time to take a step away and follow some really good advice here.)

Brandon was shocked. So he chose to take his health seriously and change his lifestyle. He had a family to live for, he had too many family members who had died before their time, he had a goal to reach a hundred years old, something no one in his family had achieved. He was only thirty-six.

The doctor offered suggestions of diets and of course two prescription medications to control cholesterol and his extremely high blood pressure. The side effects of the medications were not something he wanted to contend with, so he took a pass on the medication and went ALL IN for a healthy eating plan and a minimum of thirty minutes a day walking. He was exchanging his routine of a bowl of ice cream every night before bed for tennis shoes and low carb meals. (I will interject again, I didn't say diet because the term needs to go bye-bye. All those who struggle and really want to stop the merry-go-round and get to a normal frame need to realize it is a change in lifestyle, a new way to eat, a change in mindset — not something you do until you achieve a goal and then revert.)

Brandon began low carb eating and walking. Within the first few weeks he noticed a big drop of weight due to the water flush, this happens when carbs are reduced or eliminated. Slowly he noticed his pants fitting different. His job was located where he could go and get his blood pressure checked every noontime. He saw that coming down gradually. Soon he was moving from a thirty-minute walk to a walk/run/walk combo around his neighborhood. He still had his sweet tooth craving but found berries were sweet and the only fruit allowed on a low carb-eating plan as well as carb smart bars could stop the craving.

Fast forward ten years — both he and my daughter are exercise and wellness driven. My daughter lost a good deal working out and eating along with Brandon. Brandon dropped a hundred pounds and gained a bit in muscle mass to come in at a healthy body fat around 17-18%. They both added cross-fit training to their exercise routine. Brandon decided lifting weights was something he *wanted* to do. Now they both are enjoying a much healthier lifestyle.

When he talks to people, he offers them the following advice. If you are at that place where you know you need to do something, take a listen:

- Your why needs to be bigger than your why not. Motivation doesn't sustain, discipline is what drives you.
- The outcome, where you want to be, needs to be so important nothing, absolutely nothing, gets in the way. Think of Jesus in

the wilderness and Satan's attempt to sidetrack him. He didn't allow it. His why was BIGGER.

- See pain when muscles are sore as an achievement, but DO NOT go ALL IN at first. You will get sorer than you can tolerate and get discouraged. Start with thirty minutes of walking every single day, especially if you have a sedentary lifestyle. Advance as you are able.

- Lose the fat person mentality, quit seeing yourself in the mirror as flawed. You have been fearfully and wonderfully made. Find your way to a healthy place and embrace who you are in Christ and in health.

I loved sharing Brandon's story and I recently watched him and Christina run a half marathon. I have taken my cues from them because what they have achieved inspires me. I'm on my own journey to get where I want to be. While I have some factors physically to work around and age, I am not allowing those factors to sidetrack me. I have my bigger why, I am determined to let nothing get in the way and with small beginnings and the Lord's help I have fitness goals and clothing size goals for 2021. You can too. Join me. Let's grab a big slice of victory.

that still small **Whisper**

DAY 37
TEACH

I spent this morning early reading Matthew 13 and the different parables, seven in total. The closing verses talk about Jesus being rejected in Nazareth. Jesus had spent considerable time teaching and then returned home. When he taught in his hometown, everyone was baffled at where he gained his wisdom. Jesus had grown up there, people knew him. Joseph was a carpenter and with Mary and the other children they were nothing extraordinary.

Verse fifty-seven mentions how his hometown people were offended by him, and refused to believe in him. Because of their unbelief, Jesus only performed a few miracles there.

Isn't it sad to be the Son of God and have the power to raise the dead and yet the very people you call your closest friends (neighbors), who have known you most of your young life, who were there to watch you grow, were the very ones to reject you?

Lord, may we never be found guilty of rejecting you. Help us learn and apply all you have taught so our lives can manifest a bit of heaven here on earth. We guard every miracle as a precious event where we know you have walked ever closer to us. Amen.

The whisper I hear today is *teach*, this is defined as a means to show, explain, train, or tutor someone in how to do a task. In every parable there was something being taught and an application for our lives. Jesus told his disciples, "To those who listen to my teaching, more understanding will be given, and they will have an abundance of knowledge…" Matthew 13:12 (NLT)

I took a long look at my abundance meter today to evaluate how much understanding I have received. The scriptures teach me every time I read the Bible. Isn't the goal to keep learning for a lifetime? What we might learn and apply one day will be a steppingstone to something else we will learn in the future.

Let me share a story written by my daughter, Jennifer, a teacher.

Teach is a rather funny word, don't you think? By itself, the word is spit out of the mouth as though it were a curse. And yet, a curse couldn't be more wrong. Webster would define it as – cause to know, to guide studies, and even, to impart knowledge.

How wonderful. How life giving. How poetic. And yet, there is a teacher shortage in the United States and that's a rather curious predicament given the romantic definition.

No, I think there is more to "teach" than simply imparting knowledge. Teaching is a thing of beauty. I dare say, teaching is an art-form and not for the faint-of-heart.

Just look at Jesus' ministry in Luke nine. Jesus feeds five thousand with five loaves of bread and two fish. Peter declares Him to be the Messiah. Then Peter, James, and John witness His Transfiguration.

But look at what follows in verses thirty-seven through forty-two. I will give you the key points. After they had come down the mountain, a large crowd met Jesus. A man in the crowd called out to him to heal his son. The man told Jesus he begged the disciples to cast out the evil spirit from his son, but they couldn't do it. Jesus then pronounces in verse forty-one, "You faithless and corrupt people! How long must I be with you and put up with you?" (NLT) Jesus asked to see the boy. Jesus was unfazed at the evil spirit and instead rebuked it and healed the boy returning him well to his father.

Jesus goes from his high moment, the transfiguration, to this back-to-square-one moment. He actually asks the question, "How long must I be with you and put up with you?" Surely this thought has crossed the mind of every parent or teacher out there. As a parent or teacher, have you ever felt exasperated?

I teach middle school science. I love it. I often feel a great connection to Jesus, as a Rabbi, through my profession. Each time I encounter moments like the above, elsewhere in scripture, I understand our great teacher all the more. Not for what He must have felt in that frustrating moment (did Jesus ever roll his eyes at His disciples?) but because of what he did next.

In my profession, I often hear stories of teachers who only help students who "want to be there" or "care about their education." Ashamedly, I admit I have experienced similar thoughts. This is hardly Christ-like.

God reveals another way — He always does. Look at what Jesus did — he heals the boy. Another teachable moment accomplished.

Jesus wasn't Rabbi simply because He knew scripture. Jesus, as Rabbi, modeled every expectation in utter perfection. Through His example we are taught what it means to love, to have peace that surpasses all understanding, to thrive in the face of adversity, and so much more.

What was the result? Luke 9:43 (NLT) states "Awe gripped the people as they saw this majestic display of God's power."

I challenge you to watch for the teachable moment in your day. How is God using it to reveal His majesty in your life? How will that moment impact those you teach?

that still small *Whisper*

DAY 38
COVENANT

    This morning I turned back to the Old Testament. One of my favorite books to read is Isaiah. Chapter 54 talks about the future of Jerusalem and continues into chapter 55 with detailed information on the promises of God. Here are a few of my favorite take-a-ways from those two chapters.

- 54:10 – God's faithful and enduring love and covenant of peace and blessing will stand forever and not be broken.
- 54:11,12 – God will rebuild and fortify the city with the most precious commodities.
- 54:15 – If a nation comes to fight and is foolish enough to challenge and fight you, it is not God, and they will go down in defeat.
- 54:17 – After God has said all of this, He ends the chapter with this declaration, "…in that coming day, no weapon turned, used against you will succeed. You will silence every voice raised up to accuse you." (NLT). God will vindicate his chosen people.
- 55:3 – Listen closely and you will find life. I will make an everlasting covenant. "…I will give you all the unfailing love I

promised to David." (NLT)

- 55:6 – Seek, turn your face and attention toward the Lord while he is near and can be found.
- 55:8 – His thoughts are higher than ours. He handles things different than we do.
- 55:11 - His words, wherever they are sent, will always produce, will accomplish and will prosper everywhere He sends them.

The whisper I hear today is *covenant*, which is defined simply as an agreement. Who else makes a better commitment, contract, guarantee, promise and pledge than God? I also found a synonym for covenant; indenture. A term not used in our present time but a term which meant a lot to our ancestors.

I have an ancestor named Mary Watson. She came from Ireland and was *indentured* to a wealthy landowner in Virginia in the mid 1700s. She was tied to this owner for many years. He bought her from a soul driver for a price, and held her contract. She was contracted to work for him for a predefined number of years.

Imagine for a moment that glorious day when we discovered, through salvation how we are connected in lineage to the most famous Biblical people who have ever lived. Once your heart realizes you are descendants/children of the most treasured and protected people ever to have been living on the earth, there will be and should be a shout of joy.

Just like I would do anything to protect my family from harm and do everything I could to protect their reputation, it is also good to guard our spiritual connection and revere the majestic and powerful declarations of God, who is our Father and the provider of our inheritance. We have been bought for a price, Christ's life and blood on a cross. Dying to self fortifies Gods covenant.

Being bold and standing for Christ will always put you on the winning side and bring favor upon you and your descendants. Have you taken your stand for Christ and made him not only the ruler on the throne but also the ruler of your heart as well as that of your home, work, community, and nation?

that
still *whisper*
small

DAY 39
OBEY

During my quiet time I decided to sing and worship and got lost in the peace of the moment. There wasn't a particular passage of scripture I was drawn to read. I only wanted to pour out my love and devotion in song and wait on him to speak to my heart. I hear the whisper, *obey*. I immediately felt warmth around this whispering, and it is wonderful to be able to feel this way.

For many who have grown up in a less than perfect environment the term "obey" carries a negative connotation. It's a word that elicits many emotions and none very good. Many might even feel repulsed at its utterance. I know because that used to be me.

Like I have shared already, my childhood home life was not a warm, loving or peaceful place. I learned to obey as soon as I could walk and talk. I learned this was mandatory, or else. The "or else" usually meant all hell would break loose if I even hinted at being disobedient.

I often have wondered what willing obedience looked like when it came from a posture of love and respect. This was totally foreign to me, a concept I simply couldn't bring my mind to comprehend.

I would shudder at weddings when I heard brides and grooms pledging to love, honor, and obey. How could they make these vows and be so cheerful? For many years the motivating factor for me to "obey" came from a place of fear and torment. I knew to not obey meant wrath, punishment, and heartache. I obeyed to not be beaten.

There it was, out in the open and it was time for the salve of Jesus to be applied to this gapping, bleeding wound still raw from years of abuse. So that is what I did. I went on my face before the Lord and let him wrap my entire being in his love. I stayed in his presence until I could no longer feel the sting of every belt lashing and verbal accusation. Even to this day, when old movie reels try to play in my head, I get before the Lord and wait on him to come and comfort me.

I asked God to heal my reaction to "obey." He was quick to respond to my heart. I came to realize that obedience when done *for* someone who you love and who returns love is a wonderful thing. I obey the Lord because I love him, I want to please him and I want favor to rest on my life.

Lord, I pray for those who have suffered abuse of any fashion to get on their face before you. Bring healing though the blood of Jesus. Amen. Stay before him because he cares more deeply than you know.

I know many of you may be thinking the exact thing I have prayed about on several occasions, "Lord if you have always been there in my life where were you when (insert what you want here) was happening to me." I've asked Jesus where he was when I was a baby whose very existence was disgusting to one of my parents. Where was Jesus during every belt beating I endured as a young girl that left welts on my legs and buttocks I had to hide from teachers and friends? Where was Jesus when....

But Jesus was there. I honestly believe every painful form of abuse hurt his heart too. I will forever love God despite my painful past because the sum of it all gives me so many areas I can relate to others. I have chosen of my own free will to allow everything, even what the enemy meant for my destruction, to be a victory in Jesus. I take every painful experience and wait to see where I can give God the glory and turn it all around. Instead of being bitter I look to make someone else better. It all has made me a stronger individual and I hope a living breathing power for the greatest gift of all, LOVE.

Trust me, in my flesh there screams a cry for justice. I just have to keep that carnal flesh crucified daily because not one good thing comes from acting out of the flesh. I choose, DAILY, to walk in love, forgiveness, and to obey the one who formed me, kept me and will be my Lord for all of eternity. I call him Father, Abba.... Daddy.

that still small *whisper*

DAY 40
DECLARE, BAPTIZE, AND TESTIFY

If you have ever been to a race you know the importance of the trifecta. Get that bet right and you stand to profit exceedingly well. We have come to the end of our forty days.

I want to end our days together with a trifecta — three whispers, one for each facet of the Godhead. I wanted to spend time focusing on the Trinity.

Let's begin with, God....The Father.

My favorite Bible scripture is Psalm 91. It has been my go-to when I want to really get close to God. Every stanza is filled with power, authority, and/or promise. It speaks to how God views me and wants to protect me when I am near to Him.

I ask that you read it, and then read it again in a different translation or two. Really let the words get into your being. Picture God declaring every word over you, personally.

Most High God, I am grateful for the love you show to me and for what you do each and every day to grow our relationship. I accept and receive all your promises and want to make sure I begin each day glorifying you. Amen.

The whisper I hear today is *declare*, making a bold and assertive proclamation. I want to speak life-giving words over my family and myself. We need divine protection and provision. As you abundantly provide for us, we then have at our disposal what is needed to sow into your kingdom.

The second part of the Trinity is Jesus… the Son.

My favorite scripture about Jesus is when he arrived at the Jordan River to be baptized by John the Baptist. I can't help but think, long before when he was conceived, the Angel Gabriel appeared to Elizabeth and Mary about their intended and soon to be sons. God had miraculously given each of these women a son. The two men would take different journeys, but they meet together at the river where heaven came down and met them both. Those sons would bring so much to the world for us.

Matthew 3:15 (NLT) Jesus tells John (my notes in parenthesis), "It (speaking of his baptism) should be done, for we must carry out all that God requires (fulfill all righteousness)."

Once Jesus comes up out of the water, Heaven opens, and the Spirit of God descends and rests upon him. There comes a voice from Heaven declaring Jesus as the Son in whom God is well pleased.

Lord, how wonderful to be able to follow the model of Jesus and be baptized. Making the declaration that we desire to be in right standing with God by leaving behind, in the cleansing water, our sin nature and coming up, out of the water, to live victorious with Jesus as our savior. Amen.

The whisper is *baptize*, which symbolizes purification or regeneration. That should be enough to shout Hallelujah!

Can you remember the day you were baptized? If you haven't been you can be. It is such an exhilarating feeling and packed full of emotions. It is your outward statement to the world about the inner work of God in your life.

Take a few minutes today and recall that moment and how you felt. I'm sure you will be powerfully reenergized in your spiritual connection to the Trinity.

The final focus is the third person of the Trinity…. The Holy Spirit.

We can't negotiate this life without the Holy Spirit. He is an endless adjective in nature. The facets about Him I lean on most are as guide and comforter.

You read Acts to find the first outpouring of the Spirit on believers. Chapter 2:1-4 is worth a read and study in as many translations as you can find. Just like when Jesus was baptized there _came from heaven_ and then flames rested on each person gathered there.

Luke wrote this after his Gospel accounting; the Holy Spirit in the Christ followers was a means to perform miracles and the way in which to proclaim the Good News to the world. Performing and proclaiming are both action words and available to those in the upper room that day as well as to us for a lifetime. Isn't it thrilling?

Lord, thank you for giving us and residing in us by way of the Holy Spirit. May we guard our temple and revere His presence. Give us listening ears to hear when He speaks and guides us. May we treasure this powerful gift and use it as God intended from the time he came to rest on Jesus — the Holy Spirit was with Him and for use by Him for others. Amen.

The final whisper is _testify_ and this simply means to give an accurate account of a happening or event, and the proof of something's existence.

We, as Christians, are the world's proof that Jesus did exist and our actions through the Holy Spirit should always be pointing others to the cross. Jesus came to provide a new life for all. It was about Him, about the Father and His love for us. Jesus is sitting with the Father and will one day come again. May we do everything we can to point others to heaven as our ultimate goal. Our hope and purpose for living is to glorify Him in everything we say and do.

Let me share a final story which has elements of many of the proceeding whisperings.

Over the course of my life and in finding my purpose I have inquired of the Lord while also telling him that I would do *anything* he asked of me. I knew and was fully persuaded that the Lord would never ask more of me than I was capable of. Everything I did for him I was convinced he would also provide the strength and stamina required.

Ken and I married in 2000 and we both had been single parents for most of the 90s, each with four children. Our wedding blended a family of eight children. We were so confident when we went through our pre martial counseling, skipping the chapter on child rearing because his youngest was already a teen and the other seven children were grown. It didn't matter how we parented because there was no medical possibility for us to have an "ours" to add to the Wicks quiver.

Fast-forward three years into our new marriage. One of Ken's biological daughters had left home, was involved in drugs and living on the streets. She had also gotten pregnant. We had no contact with her or knowledge of even her exact physical whereabouts.

Ken got the call that would change our lives forever. His daughter had delivered a drug baby and Child Protective Services had taken possession of the 4 lb. 4 oz. baby girl. The caseworker wanted to know if Ken wanted the baby.

I still remember the day he walked into our home, white as a sheet and speechless. He proceeded to tell me the whole conversation with the CPS worker and also stated this was not something he wanted to do, all over again. He just couldn't fathom being a parent to an infant at his age. For him the situation was a closed book. When I inquired as to what the

CPS worker mentioned, he said, "There is a hearing later in the week and we could attend the proceedings."

I was quick to remind Ken that he was not a single dad any longer and that "we" were a couple and would do only as the Lord directed us. I asked him, "What has the Lord told you to do?" His response was he hadn't prayed about it. To which I told him, rather emphatically, to do so immediately. I would honor and stand by whatever the Lord told him to do.

As he disappeared to the bedroom to pray, I shot a statement to the Lord, which went exactly like this, "Lord that baby is our family, she didn't ask to be born and deserves to be with us and not a foster to adopt home. Now get in there and tell that man what to do."

I was surprised when Ken reappeared from the bedroom and said he felt the Lord telling him to go to court and he would know what to do when he got there. He was still leaning toward the baby staying with the foster home if we could determine it was a loving, caring place.

I was anxious because I had told my husband I would support his decision. You see the test for me was if I could keep my mouth out of it and let the Lord do the driving. This was a huge step for my rather controlling personality.

We both prayed and went to the court hearing. We found out the foster to adopt home was lovely and the mother there was already bonding with the baby girl. Ken was satisfied as we went into court. I was aching inside.

Then, in a twist, the biological paternal family made a request to have the baby removed from foster care and brought to their home. There was a heavy drug influence there as well as some other offenses to be considered by the authorities before changing the home placement for the infant. My husband asked the CPS worker if this would be possible and she could only state that if a family member passed the home study, the child would be moved. AT THAT MOMENT my husband knew what he had to do. He shot to his feet and told the judge we wanted to be home studied for possible placement. I about exploded with relief.

It took about four weeks, but in the end, we were awarded the baby and she came to live with us at eight weeks old. (See how funny God is? That chapter on parenting we skipped in counseling before marriage was now a reality. What we thought impossible, God decided to have the final word.)

The baby girl, Nicole is now seventeen and a very gifted young woman. I can see the Lord's favor on and through her life. She chases hard after Jesus and has committed her life to Him.

When she was five, I had a co-worker tell me that she could see us ministering together. I tucked that away not knowing how or what that would look like. We both did many years of community theater together acting on stage and Nicole has excelled in the arts. Although we have bonded more in our theater involvement, I didn't think this was the "ministering" my co-worker mentioned years prior.

In a dramatic turn of events, right when Nicole was really shining onstage as a talented triple threat, she suffered a debilitating anxiety attack. It has been something she worked daily to overcome, and it has also sidelined her from the on-stage portion of theater.

While this has been sad for us as parents and for her personally, I began to see another hand of God. This time it centered on teens. Nicole could identify with many her age who suffered emotional battles. Covid and the isolation surrounding this virus has only made things worse for these most vulnerable teens.

Now I will not profess to know, ever, all about the now teen culture with Snapchat, Tiktok and Instagram, but I am savvy enough to know the

Lord's leading when I feel it. Just like I was quick to sew over nine-hundred masks in March 2020 when our world experienced a global pandemic. I could feel the surging in my spirit to take this "Whispering family" and grow it for the teens. Just like I desire for everyone to hear their own whispers each and every day I also wanted to have a group of whispering teens who will whisper to other teens. So that suggestion from a friend twelve years ago about us working together in ministry has a very real goal on the near horizon. Look for book two in this series to be one every teen will want to have in their hands.

If you want to know how the parenting of Nicole went with that skipped chapter, yes Ken and I parent completely different, and our marriage has survived despite those differences. Thanks to God's grace, we are about to celebrate Nicole's eighteenth birthday in 2021. I think she turned out to be a terrific young woman with a wonderful future.

So yes, the Lord has provided strength and stamina for me to raise another child the past eighteen years and for that I am beyond grateful. It has not been easy. I tell people that it is a very different experience raising a child when you are in your fifties and sixties instead of your twenties and thirties. There have been unique challenges I never thought would be part of my life. One in particular, I never saw myself pushing a stroller in the mall alongside my daughter pushing my grandchild in hers. I want to hope I had more wisdom for the second go around parenting adventure. Only heaven knows if that's a fact. I simply answered a call and gave it my best.

that still small *whisper*

FINAL THOUGHTS

I'm grateful for all these "whisperings" and how they have impacted my life. My hope and prayer is that every reader who took this 40 day journey has gained a slice of heaven for their life.

Many people set goals and make resolutions. I prefer to work on growth and depth. I want to always be learning and therefore growing and hopefully making any shallow areas of life deeper and richer.

I desire to have the world hear their own unique whispers and be a whisperer for others, proving that positives far outweigh the negatives in life. There is nothing impossible with God in us, when our lives are committed to help those around us.

I love being a Whisperer and hope you will become one too.

that still small *Whisper*

ABOUT THE AUTHOR

Carla has been a Christian for over half her life and has a passion for God's Word. She coupled this fervor with a concentration on prayer. Being open and vulnerable about the good and bad experiences of life has been her focus. Her biblical education has spanned forty-six years including many correspondence courses, bible studies (including one's she has written and lead), attending conventions, speaking at retreats/conferences, and Pastoral and Stephen Ministry classes. She has devoted herself to expand knowledge and mature in the faith. She is an advocate for life-long learning.

She is a Veteran of the USAF, retired Registered Dental Hygienist, and Gold Star Mother. She and has been freelance writing and blogging for several years. Her most recent works include a novel, Summer at Eagle Crest Drive, and co-authoring The Potluck Club—the play.

Having grown up in Kansas, she moved twenty-three years ago and now calls Ft. Worth, Texas home. She is married to her husband Ken and homeschooling their daughter Nicole who is a junior in high school. She is mother of nine and grandmother of twelve. You can reach Carla for media requests, autographed copies, and individual orders at 40whispers@gmail.com.

www.ingramcontent.com/pod-product-compliance
Lightning Source LLC
Chambersburg PA
CBHW071459080526
44587CB00014B/2151